What Some are Saying about IRIS

Oh, how I love this woman. I loved her before I ever met her—and even more after that! Her story, her faith, and her faithfulness are such a testimony of God's gracious and thorough work of redemption. You'll want to read and share *IRIS: Trophy of Grace,* and then you'll want to have her come and share in person. Or, get the DVD we had the privilege of filming at Precept Ministries International. You're going to love my precious friend and her husband and you'll find your heart stirred to reach out to the seemingly unreachable—but for the grace of God

—**Kay Arthur:** *Precept Ministries International*

Iris Blue's life is the most inspiring story that could be told! Against all odds, with nothing to indicate there was even a glimpse of hope, God's powerful grace entered her life and completely transformed her. Ron Owens has captured the drama of this miracle in compelling style. It is a must read!

—**Jimmy Draper:** President Emeritus, *LifeWay Christian Resources* Nashville, TN

The first time I heard Iris' story, tears flowed as I was reminded afresh of the unabandoned and outrageous grace our God extends. I was compelled to get on my knees and worship God for, not just what He had done in her life, but for what He'd done in mine. Everyone needs to hear the incredible testimony told in the pages of this book. With each chapter you will unearth more of the glorious redemption that was available to Iris and is, at this very moment, available to you.

—**Priscilla Shirer:** Teacher, *Going Beyond Ministries,* Dallas Texas

Already acclaimed for his unique ability to capture the essence of life in biographical form, Ron Owens now shares with us another remarkable story of God's grace—*Iris: Trophy of Grace.* This is the true account of Iris Urrey Blue, a living illustration of God's miraculous power. You will find yourself captivated by the fresh, transparent and wholesome presentation of a life that had every chance of failure and virtually none for success—until her meeting with Jesus changed everything. If you liked *They Could Not Stop the Music* and *Manley Beasley: Man of Faith, Instrument of Revival,* you will love reading this book.

—**Tom Elliff:** President of *Living in the Word Ministries,* author, missionary

Your reading of *IRIS: Trophy of Grace*, will be more beneficial and blessed of the Lord if you read it as a sequel to *Manley Beasley: Man of Faith, Instrument of Revival*, another biography by Ron Owens. In the first paragraph of Iris' *Prelude* she says it all: *"God brought Bro. Manley into my life to teach me and show me, by his life, what living by faith really is."* What a legacy Manley left through his investment in Iris' life. As you read this book you will experience first hand the biblical mandate that the Apostle Paul gave to Timothy: *"The things you have learned from me entrust to others, who are faithful."* Iris, you learned well and you are faithfully passing it on. All glory to our wonderful Lord!

> —**Joe Ann Shelton:** *Associates in Accomplishment*, Amarillo, Texas

This book, *IRIS: Trophy of Grace*, is a must read if you want to know God better. Ron Owens leads us into a world we've never known so we can experience the depth of God's love, grace and power through His work in Iris Blue. You will laugh, cry and praise God as He transforms this Iris into a flower that the glory of Solomon could not surpass. You owe it to yourself to read this book. You won't be able to stop talking about it.

> —**Avery Willis:** Executive Director of the *International Orality Network*, author and missionary

My first encounter with Iris was hearing her story at the Texas Evangelism Conference. Tears filled my eyes as I heard of God's faithfulness and grace in her. Ron Owens' account of her walk with Jesus will thrill and encourage you. It is like reading from the life of one in the Gospels where Jesus passed by and gave a transforming touch. Read this book and pass it on to someone who needs a message of hope.

> —**Ted Traylor:** Pastor, *Olive Baptist Church*, Pensacola, Florida

Ron Owens has once again taken us inside the life of one of God's New Creations. The life of Iris Urrey Blue gives us a word picture of 2 Corinthians 5:17. Her life defines what a new creation (species) should look like. This is a "must read" for the Body of Christ as we witness her evolution from tragedy to triumph.

> —**Mack Kearney:** President. *Gospel Harvesters International*, Hurst, Texas

The story God used to change my life is found in this book. Ron has truly captured the "essence" of Iris, especially after she gave her life to Christ. I believe that all who read it will not only be blessed but will be drawn to love Christ for the first time or to love Him more. I recommend this book to everyone. It will encourage you, change you and motivate you because it's all about Jesus and His love for us, no matter who we are or what we've done. Meet Him in this book.

> —**Paula Edney:** College basketball coach; Coach of the women's *Athletes in Action* team for five years and Head Coach of the 1985 *USA Pan Am Games* team

An incredible story of God's amazing grace—that sums up *Iris: Trophy of Grace!* Ron Owens has done a masterful job of using humor, emotion and biblical truth to tell the story of God's transforming work in the life of Iris Blue. Her story is simply powerful, and the Kingdom will be enhanced having it available in print. In a culture where God's miraculous work is often explained away or marginalized, this book reminds us that He is still in the life-changing business! This must-read story of redemption will reignite your passion to share Christ with everyone around you.

> —**L. Lavon Gray:** Minister of Music & Worship, *First Baptist Church,* Jackson, MS

Iris Blue is a powerful witness to God's redemptive love. Hers is a story that should be mandatory reading for both young and old. We were thrilled to welcome Iris into our home and to Faith Baptist Church in Kaiserslautern, Germany. We were pleased to have been a part of her ministry. Our children used to enjoy sitting on her lap and none of us will ever forget her abounding joy that touched everyone around her. Ron Owens has done a magnificent job of capturing this marvelous story of salvation. It will be a blessing to all who read it.

> —**Robert (Bob) Ferguson:** Retired *European Baptist Convention* pastor and former EBC president

Webster's dictionary defines "Iris" as *the goddess of the rainbow, the messenger of the gods.* To those who know her, Iris Urrey Blue is a beautiful flower, beautiful name and beautiful messenger of the only true God. I have never met a more transparent Christian than Iris. It is refreshing to be in her presence. She has never lost the wonder of God's love and grace. Thank you, Ron, for bringing this dynamic testimony to this present generation.

> —**Barbara O'Chester:** Founder and retired director of the *Great Hills Ladies Retreat Ministry,* Austin, TX

Iris Blue is a trophy of the marvelous grace of God. I have heard her testimony many times and it never fails to stir my heart for soul-winning. She has the

Spirit of our Lord radiating from her changed life. You will be reminded that the blood of Jesus covers it all as you read how she was redeemed from the House of Shame and placed into the House of Fame—the Lamb's Book of Life. Read and be blessed!

—**Sonny Holland:** Evangelist, *Sonny Holland Ministries,* Clinton, LA

Iris exemplifies living by faith through her daily walk with Jesus. I have watched her through the years as she has trusted Him spiritually, financially, emotionally and in her daily relationships. She has personally witnessed Jesus' unfailing love since the moment she knelt down on that Houston sidewalk and received Jesus as her Bridegroom. This book reflects her awesome growth through a most intriguing relationship with her Savior.

—**Catherine Morris:** *Medical Doctor,* Canton, Georgia

Ron Owens has captured in this story of Iris Blue the only true and permanent re-habilitation program—receiving Jesus Christ as Savior. During my years as a Federal Prison Warden I managed many correctional re-habilitation programs and experienced that when convicts received Christ as their Savior true re-habilitation took place. As good as education, self-help groups and job training programs were, these could only develop smarter and more capable convicts, whereas, Jesus Christ transformed them from the inside out.

—**J. Allman:** Federal Prison Warden, retired

IRIS

Trophy of Grace

*The miraculous story of Iris Urrey Blue,
the "incorrigible" who encountered
the irresistible force of God's
transforming power.*

Ron Owens
with
Iris Urrey Blue

Published by
Innovo Publishing, LLC
InnovoPublishing.com
1-888-546-2111

Providing Full-Service Publishing Services for
Christian Authors, Artists & Organizations: Hardbacks, Paperbacks,
eBooks, Audiobooks, Music & Film

IRIS TROPHY OF GRACE

Library of Congress Control Number: 20109-34259
ISBN: 978-1-61314-342-1

Revised Cover Design & Revised Interior Layout: Innovo Publishing, LLC

Printed in the United States of America

U.S. Printing History

First Edition: 2009
Second Edition: August 2016

Foreword

When I think of changed lives, one of the very first names that comes to mind is that of Iris Blue. I honestly believe that Iris has experienced as much life-change as any lady I have ever met. To believe that one day, in her own words, she *"knelt down a tramp and stood up a lady,"* on the sidewalk in front of her bar, *The Inferno,* where she could feel the vibrations of the music from the inside, is difficult to grasp but, no truer words have been spoken. This lady was radically changed.

I have never heard Iris give her testimony that it did not move me to tears and I can honestly say that I have never heard her share that I did not witness radical change take place in someone's life. To say that Iris Blue walks the walk may be the understatement of the new millennium. I am grateful that we have this example of authenticity in the 21st century. Iris is a woman who is real and exemplifies the life of the Lord Jesus Christ like few I have met in my 36 years of following God's Son.

I believe this book will be one that will so inspire, encourage and bless your heart in such a deep way that you will find yourself buying additional copies to pass along to people who you know would be encouraged, blessed or changed as a result of reading it. I can hardly wait for this volume to be available so I can put my heart around it as it is placed in my hand to once again be encouraged by Iris' story that has always warmed my heart. People love stories with good endings and this is one of those that will move you into action. It will mobilize you to reach out, not only to your community and those you think of as you are reading the book, but to the nations.

If there were another word I would attempt to use to describe Iris it would be the word, balanced. She has an unbelievable capacity for hospitality which is translated into loving strangers. Her home has always been a place where the love of Jesus has flowed so freely to those she is serving, whether it is a prostitute she has met on the street or a gang leader she is trying to influence with the gospel.

Another word that could be used to describe Iris Blue is *uniqueness.* There are peculiarities about this lady that separate her from others. The best way I can say it is that she seems to stand head and shoulders above the average Christian. I realize that in the context of God's standards that this is not necessarily true but, in Iris you see a woman who is devoted, in what some may say, extreme ways, to bringing all she comes in contact with to the foot of the cross. I guess what I'm trying to say is that my life has been radically influenced by Iris Blue, and as you read her story you'll understand why.

—Johnny Hunt
Pastor, First Baptist Church of Woodstock, Georgia
President of the Southern Baptist Convention (2008-2010)

Acknowledgements

THANK YOU, Iris, for the privilege of writing your incredible story, and thanks to Duane (Blue), Denim and Punkin, Iris' "little sister," who helped immeasurably in recalling times and events, adding their own perspective to what has taken place over the years.

Special thanks to:

• Johnny Hunt for writing the Foreword

• those who faithfully prayed over the course of the research and writing

• friends who listened to reading after reading and who offered their constructive criticism

• to my wife, Patricia, whose counsel, suggestions and encouragement helped make this book what it is

• my son, Jeff, for his work in editing and formatting the photo section for a father who knows *zilch* about such things

• those who not only read the manuscript but took the time to respond with their encouraging remarks about the book and how Iris' life has impacted theirs

• *And most of all,* to our miracle-working God whose grace reached down to a kneeling, repentant ex-con on a Houston sidewalk and transformed her into a *New Creation* in Christ.

Table of Contents

Introduction

This is the story of one of God's children who truly understands the meaning of what John Newton wrote many years ago, *"I once was lost but now am found, was blind but now I see."* Though reared in a Christian home and being expected to do all the things that a "church family" child should do, rebellion was simmering just below the surface. At the age of thirteen it erupted— Iris Urrey ran away from home. This was but the beginning of a life that would become increasingly involved in drugs, prostitution and other criminal activities. Being arrested, jailed and released, had become routine for this teenager until, at the age of seventeen, she was arrested for armed robbery. With her history of drugs and crime, the authorities worked the system and were able to hold her over until her 18th birthday so she could be tried as an adult.

"So what," was her attitude. *"If this is to be part of the life I've chosen to live— no big deal."* Iris found herself heading down the wide road that leads to destruction and she couldn't get off. She was unable to resist temptation, she was living only for the moment, without any thought of her future. A casual observer would have written her off. *"No hope for that girl."* But God was not a casual observer. He had already written the future chapters of Iris' life; chapters that she would never have thought to write herself; chapters she would never have even dared to dream.

Years in prison, solitary confinements, released back into society to immediately return to the lifestyle that had led to her incarceration, she was headed toward the same tragic ending so many of her friends would meet. But this was not to be for Iris Urrey. Pursuing her, every step of the way, in and out of prison, in the middle of heroin highs and robberies, was her Creator, who in eternity past had devised a plan that would eventually turn this "incorrigible rebel" into one of His beautiful trophies of grace. As hard as she tried, she could not hide from Him. He was always there.

But this is not only a story of grace and redemption, it is the story of a world-wide ministry that has found this longest serving *Mission Service Corps Volunteer* with the Southern Baptist *North American Mission Board*, sitting beside top military brass at a NATO function one day, then serving tea and cookies to German prostitutes on a cold wintry afternoon, the next. It is the story of perseverance in the face of obstacles placed in her way by well-meaning fellow believers who sometimes had difficulty in accepting her non-traditional approaches to reaching the disenfranchised. Through discouragements and failures, through losses and gains, this unconventional "saint" pressed on, and still presses on, by faith, toward the prize of her high calling in Christ Jesus.

Finally, this book is more than a history of Iris; it addresses many life issues that are common to us all, and in her unique way Iris provides answers out of her own personal walk with her Lord. The impact she has had on countless lives over the years is affirmed in the tributes and testimonies recorded in these pages.

—Ron Owens
January, 2010

A Word from Iris

I'm so thankful that Bro. Ron has been able to tell the story of my vulgar and dark past in such a way that brings glory to Jesus and not to sin. Our hearts have been torn as we've tried to put together facts without causing embarrassment to the reader, but for those who are reading this book and are living a wicked life right now, there is enough information for you to read between the lines and realize how far Jesus' forgiveness can reach. You know what I mean. And for those of you who can't really identify with the garbage I was in, you can still know that Jesus can reach you wherever you are, and, He can keep you free from going where I used to be. Amen? Amen!

Since I met Jesus, my life's message has been the message of faith. That is why I am so blown away that my story is following Bro. Manley Beasley's biography. He is the man the Lord Jesus brought into my life when I was a brand new Christian, to teach me by his life what living by faith really is.

Seeing people come to Jesus by faith, to this "so great salvation," is the most thrilling thing I know. It did not take me long to discover, however, that just wanting someone to be saved, or even just witnessing to them was not going to do the job. Faith is what is needed. Faith was what I needed to be a real witness, and faith is what they needed to respond to the Holy Spirit. But even after having faith for my own salvation I found that I could still feel lost, I could still feel that I was not forgiven, so I had to make a choice to go on accepting my salvation by faith and accepting my forgiveness. There are a lot of people living below what God has provided for them in salvation, because of unbelief (Psalm 103:12).

But, most of the time when people talk about living by faith they are thinking about money. Money is a big part of living by faith, but the Bible tells us that without faith it is impossible to please God in any area of life (Hebrews 11:6). When I start a day, if my desire is to please the Lord Jesus, I present myself to Him knowing that He has already walked where I am going to go. So, by faith, I can touch the untouchable, love the unlovable, and give when it sometimes doesn't seem to make sense.

When I was first saved I knew that there had to be a better way to be supported than to send out letters listing my needs. I did send a letter out one time, however, asking people to please meet my need. I told them that my need was that they stop asking me what my need was! I said: *"I am first of all a woman and what I think I need may not always match what the Lord thinks I need, so I ask you to pray, and when you do, you may get instructions that do not make sense, but when you are obedient to Him just act in faith on what He tells you."*

The only explanation for how my husband Blue and I have ministered around the world, in both hemispheres, is faith, and it all started when I began going places with Bro. Manley and Marthé. He made me trust the Lord for how I would get there and how the Lord was going to use me when I arrived. One of my first big adventures in faith was the time he told me that I was to go with him and Marthé to Alaska for a meeting. He said: *"As bad as I want to, the Lord told me not to buy your ticket, so you are going to have to trust Him yourself."* I was still crawling in the kind of faith Bro. Manley taught, but I thought I could trust the Lord for my ticket from Houston to Fairbanks.

I was directing the girl's home in Pasadena, Texas at that time, and with all I was having to trust the Lord for there, I began wondering if I would really get to go to Alaska. Bro. Manley would call and ask me if I was going, and I would give an *"I hope so...I think so,"* answer. He'd say: *"You can't get there on hope or think-so faith."* Then one day a lady donated several boxes of clothes to the girls home and as we were going through them I found a pair of tall ladies "long-handles" (thermal underwear) with little pink bows all over them. If they had been men's long-handles I would have laid them aside and not thought anything about them. But, pink bows? It suddenly dawned on me that I would never use "long-handles" in Houston, Texas, so I ran to the phone and called Bro. Manley. I shouted into the phone: *"I'm going to Alaska! I'm going to Alaska!" Well, sister, how do you know?"* he asked, thinking that I was going to say that I hoped I was going. I said, *"because I don't need long-handles in Houston."* I went to Alaska.

Praise the Lord Jesus! At the time of this writing I have been saved, delivered, plowed up, set free, for 33 years! I can truly say that *"I have been young and now am old; yet I have not seen the righteous forsaken nor his seed begging bread"* (Psalm 37:25). Beyond a shadow of doubt, if I had not met Jesus when I was young, the way I was living, I would not have gotten old.

I pray this book will be a blessing to you in your faith walk, because either you need to make that first step of faith to receive Jesus as your Savior or, you already know Him and your faith needs a boost. He never changes, and I am proof that, *"He who hath begun a good work in you (and in me) will perform it until the day of Jesus Christ"* (Philippians1:6).

Part One

The Rebellious Years

"Those who rebel against the light;
They do not know its ways
or abide in its paths."
(Job 24:13)

Department of Corrections, Goree Unit, Huntsville, Texas

"But Mama's not going to be able to come way up here to Goree"

It's about a ninety minute drive north on Interstate 45 from the south side of Houston to Huntsville, Texas—ninety minutes from the Harris County Courthouse to the Goree Unit of the Texas Department of Corrections. She had just been sentenced, shackled by handcuffs and leg irons and pushed into a paddy wagon. Now, convicted felon, Iris Urrey, would have 90 minutes to reflect on what had been happening during the nine months since her arrest for armed robbery. There was one thing for certain; she was glad the Harris County Jail experience was behind her.

From the time they'd locked her up to the time she heard the judge sentence her to seven more years, Iris had had a running battle with the jail guards who tried to control her. She was constantly fighting. The truth was, she never backed down from a good fight, she looked for fights, and in her own words, *"was so ornery that it was not long before they began putting me in the "hole."*

"This next place can't be as bad as where I've been," she thought, as the paddy wagon drove north on Interstate 45. She remembered how hard it had been to sleep in "the hole," curling her 6' 3" body around the 4' square space that had no mat, no blanket and no pillow. Now, as they approached Huntsville and were turning on to Hwy 75 where the Goree women's prison unit was located, Iris began wondering how often her Daddy would be willing to make the 150 mile roundtrip to visit her. The last thing he had said as he watched his

3

daughter being led off in shackles, was; *"I'll be coming to see you as soon as I get the visitation schedule."* She figured he would at least try. He had never missed a visitation day during the nine months she'd been in the Harris County jail, though on many of those visits, when she was in segregation, he was not able to see her. That had not deterred him, however. Every week on visitation day Pat Urrey had been there with the exact items he was permitted to bring his daughter, including $18.00 every second visit. *"But now...will he...?*

Iris thought of her mother and how badly she had treated her. When she was in the Harris County jail, her mother, Mama, would ride the bus all the way across town to often be told that her daughter was in segregation and could not be seen. One time, as her mother was walking toward the jail, she heard Iris shouting through the bars of her 4th floor cell window asking her to go to Foleys to buy some crazy game and to pick up as many Edgar Casey books as she could find. Her mother walked 16 blocks, each way, to do what Iris had asked her to do. *"But Mama's probably not going to be able to come way up here to Goree."*

Her father had not let Iris' mother attend the sentencing. He felt it would be too hard on her. He did, however, take her younger sister, Punkin,[1] with him, hoping it would put a scare into his youngest daughter who was already following in her big sister's footsteps. What Iris didn't know was that her mother would live in denial for the next seven years, doing her best to keep what was happening to Iris a secret from her friends, her church, and even relatives. When asked what Iris was doing, she'd tell people that she had moved to San Antonio to work in the Coca Cola Bottling Company. They would not press her for more information, as they all knew the truth. They had read about it in the newspapers.

Goree was at that time an all-female unit, originally established in the early 1900's. Twenty years prior to Iris' arrival it had become famous, from coast to coast, when eight women inmates, all under the age of thirty, put together a Country Western singing group that became known as *The Goree Girls*. Fort Worth radio station, WBAP, heard about them and arranged to use them on a public service program called, *Thirty Minutes Behind the Walls*. The *Goree Girls*[2] became an overnight sensation as they were broadcast on the Ft. Worth clear channel station all across America. For the next three years, every Wednesday night from ten to ten-thirty, central time, the program averaged a weekly radio audience of over 7 million listeners, while in excess of 100,000 letters a year poured into the Goree prison office.

Who knows but that Iris might have fit in with the *Goree Girls* back then. She was born with a strong, beautiful, God-given singing voice, but now, as she was about to drive through the prison gate, she had no song to sing. She would not find the song she was born to sing for another nine years, and Goree was to become anything but a place of music for her.

From Bad to Worse

"I didn't start out wanting to be bad. I had normal dreams and ambitions, just like every other kid. I wanted my mama and daddy to be proud of me. I wanted to make straight A's in school, to one day be a wife, a mother, and maybe even a nurse."

Iris grew up in Houston, Texas, in the 1950's. Her father, Pat Urrey, was a moral, God-fearing man. He was a good father and did everything he could to provide for the family, and usually they got all that they needed and most of what they wanted. Her mother was a stay-at-home mom who loved her children and was not ashamed to show it, so Iris didn't have any of the traditional excuses for turning out the way she did. She didn't come from a broken or abusive home. The Urrey's were neither rich nor poor; they were right in the middle, and that, it is said, is the best place to be.

There were four children in the Urrey family. Iris' older brother, Ernest, whom they called Jug, and her older sister Rebecca, who was nicknamed Jo, were the good kids. They were the kind of children parents brag about with their *My Child is an Honor Student* bumper stickers. On the other hand, Iris, whom they called Stinker, and her younger sister, Evelyn, better known as Punkin, were the rebellious ones.

"There were no bumper stickers for our kind," says Iris, "unless it was: *My Kid Can Whup Your Honor Student.*"

Iris can't remember when she wasn't looking for some kind of trouble. "Mama and daddy could draw an imaginary line around the yard for Ernest and Rebecca and they wouldn't cross it, but they had to put up a fence for me because I'd wander off or run away. Sometimes, just to embarrass my mama, I'd go out in the yard and make such a racket that the neighbors would come out to see what was happening.

"I remember climbing a tree one day and laughing as my parents and neighbors yelled, whistled and searched everywhere for me. Another time, I stood at the front door and held it closed with my foot as I yanked on it, acting as though it was locked, while screaming, *'Mama, PLEASE let me in. PLEASE, Mama, PLEASE let me in.'* I screamed until the neighbors came running out. My Mama was so embarrassed."

As time passed, Iris learned that if she kept pushing her mother, bugging her, that she would often end up getting her way, such as the time when she wanted to hang out with a bunch of kids at a railroad grain yard that was in their neighborhood. It was a dangerous place to play, and she knew it. A young boy had actually been killed in a freak accident some months before. Her mother said *"no,"* but Iris kept on her, kept on her, until she finally gave in. *"OK, but just for thirty minutes."* Iris recalls how, in that moment, she realized that if she kept pressing, kept pushing, she could manipulate her mother.

The Urrey family went to church every Sunday. They sat in the second row and the children were taught to listen to the preacher and to take notes on his sermon. They always attended Vacation Bible School, made the noodle necklaces, memorized Bible verses and learned a skit. Then on Friday night all the parents would come to eat cookies and watch their little darlings do their program,

Iris remembers those programs as a child. *"We'd do our skit, pick our noses, pull up our skirts, wave to our moms and dads, then sit down near the front. I didn't know it then, but now I realize that those programs are as much to hook daddy into coming as they are for the children. He'd come to see his kids perform."*

Iris recalls one particular Vacation Bible School when she was a little girl. A visiting preacher had been invited by the pastor to close out the event with an evangelistic sermon. He preached on hell.

"To preach on hell is important and necessary," Iris reminds us. "Jesus spoke more about hell than heaven, but we must be careful that we not use scare tactics. You can't scare somebody out of hell; they must be born again.

"Well, this evangelist spit and shouted and the way the lights shone on him it almost looked like he was spewing fire. He preached for 45 minutes and the longer he preached the hotter the building seemed to get. He talked about worms not dying and every time he said 'HELL,' he'd hit the pulpit and say: *'AND-duh GGGOD-duh'* All us kids inhaled and gasped, *'Uuuhhh!'* This evangelist had jowls and he really got our attention.

"At the end of his sermon he yelled, *'NOW-uh! How many of you children want to go to HELL-uh?'* *'Good night,'* I thought. *'Who would have to think about that? Who's going to say, give me until next week and I'll let you know.'* I can't think of anyone saying, *'I want to go there.'* He had us bow our heads. *'Nobody looking,'* he said. *'Keep your heads bowed and your eyes closed.'* But I was too scared to close my eyes. I sat there staring at him.

"*'NOW-uh,'* he roared, as he snapped his fingers. *'If you don't want to go to HELL-uh, come on down.'* I started crying. I was terrified. It is one thing to cry when your dog gets run over, but if you cry in church your mama thinks you are sincere and got saved. I ran down front with all the other kids. I still was afraid to close my eyes and as I looked around I saw the evangelist's wife counting all the people who had come forward. *"One, two, three…"* It must have been time for their newsletter.

"I said a little prayer at the altar and two weeks later I was baptized and became a member of the church. From that time on everyone believed I was a Christian, no matter what was happening in my life. Whenever I'd get into trouble my mama would say that I was just out of fellowship and needed to rededicate my life to the Lord. In reality, I was lost and headed for hell."

Manley Beasley, Iris' mentor and father in the faith, had a deep concern about counterfeit conversions. In his booklet, *Is Your Salvation Real or Counterfeit3*, he says:

"One of the greatest tragedies in the world today is the fact that many professing Christians have a religion to live by—but it is not going to do when it comes time to die. It is sobering to think that in many of our churches we have taught our children, from a very early age, to believe in Jesus and to love Him, but we have

never taught them that there is a difference between intellectual belief and the belief that saves.

"We must teach them that they are totally incapable of believing in Jesus and loving Him until, by the power of the Holy Spirit, they have seen themselves as sinners and in repentance have committed themselves to the person of Jesus as Lord and Master of their lives."

Seventeen years passed before Iris would understand this. Seventeen years with her name recorded on a church role. Seventeen years before her name would be entered into the *Lamb's Book of Life*.

Rebellion

Rebellion often starts at a very young age. You don't have to teach a child to whine and cry or push a parent to the limit. Everyone is born with a basic rebellious sin nature.

"My rebellion started out small." Iris remembers. "I would make this *TKK* sound as I flicked my tongue against the back of my front teeth. Even though it wasn't a word, I knew what it meant. It had the same meaning as rolling your eyes or flipping your hair. This simple sound worked very well for me. Can you imagine someone asking me why I was in trouble?

"'Well, I made a noise.'
'You made a noise? Sure... You're being punished for making a noise!'"

But for Iris, making the *TKK* sound was just the first step. It can happen in any home. It's called a bad attitude. It's called being sassy. It starts small, then it grows. Sin never stands still.

"One day when my mama told me to clean my room I made the *TKK* sound and walked away. I thought: *Some day I'm going to be my own boss and nobody is going to tell me what to do.'* I wanted to cuss and scream but I knew that if I did, I'd get into big trouble so, for now, I'll just make the *TKK* sound.'

"Mama said. *'I think you're showing a bad attitude when you make that sound.'* *'Well, I may make that sound but at least I don't cuss like the daughter of the woman you pray with on Thursdays.'*

"Parents love to think that their children are just a little bit better than the children of other parents. I could always find someone worse than I was. Everywhere I go, whether in church, a bar, or a prison, people are always comparing themselves to others. *'Well...I might do this, but I don't do that. Honey, this isn't as bad as she's doing.'* And with each comparison we draw a new boundary line, just a little farther out.

"One day I dropped something on my foot and mama heard a bad word fly out of my mouth. *'Well, I may TKK and cuss, but I don't smoke.'* I had stepped over the *TKK* line and expanded my boundaries to include cussing. Soon after that I crossed the cussing line and drew the line at smoking. With each new line I crossed I'd look back and say: *'That wasn't so bad after all.'*

Consequences of a poor self image

As a twelve year old Iris was the biggest kid in school. At 6' 3" she towered over everyone else. She developed a serious complex about her size, and because she was so big the boys never looked at her as the girlfriend type. One time when she tried to flirt and look sexy, she leaned up against a locker, which she says, almost fell in. The only time she got to hold hands with boys was when she'd arm-wrestle them. This made them even less interested in her because she always won.

Iris recalls the little boy she had a crush on in elementary school. "I think he may have been afraid that I was going to crush him. Anyway, one day he came up to me and said: *'Listen, I need to ask you something.'* Because he sounded nervous I thought, *'I bet he is going to ask me if I'll go steady with him.'*
"'*Sure, what?*' I said.
'Will you carry me piggy back?'
"My heart sank. *'Piggyback?'* I wanted to scream, *'NO! My dream is that you'll want to carry my books, that you'll open the door for me...'* All I wanted was to be treated like I was valuable. I wanted to be treated as a lady. I wanted someone to think I was special. But the little computer in my head said: *'That's not going to happen. You see who gets to hold hands with the boys. It's those itty-bitty cute girls.'*
"I wanted to cry, but I didn't want anyone to see the tears. I had already learned, even in church, to not let anybody know what's really going on inside. Put a smile on your face and act like everything is OK.

"I was brokenhearted. I felt rejected. I ran home and asked my mother, *'Why am I so big? Is there a pill I can take? Is there an operation or something? I feel like a freak.'* Mama reached as deeply into herself as she could and gave the best answer she knew to give.

"'Honey, God made you that way.'

"'You're kidding,' I thought. *'And you want me to worship Him? No wonder everyone looks so sad in church. God must have pulled a dirty trick on them all.'* I made a deliberate decision at that young age that I didn't like God and was not going to have anything to do with Him."

It was at this point Iris started to compromise her dreams. She gave up on being treated as a lady and started to draw boundary lines further and further out. By the time she had made it to eighth grade her life was out of control and she had no idea how to handle it. She'd get strung out on drugs, kicked out of one school after the other—seven schools in all. She was in and out of jail, admitted to a psychiatric hospital, released, just to start the cycle all over again.

"My parents paid thousands of dollars for psychological testing. I was admitted to a private sanitarium three times. Each time I would stay about a month. They'd keep me off of heroin but I would stay just as high on their prescription drugs. The doctors finally determined that I was not insane. They said my problem was that I had a 'don't care attitude.' They were right. If my parents threatened to whup me I'd say: *'Go ahead. Whup me. Ground me. Do whatever you want. I don't care.'*

Iris' parents sent her to live with an aunt whom they thought could straighten her out if anyone could. Iris made promises, with good intentions. Her aunt and uncle bought all the school supplies she would need to attend yet another school. They even bought her a special kind of bathing suit, bathing cap and gym suit. The night before her first day at school her uncle said: *"Now, here is the deal. If you mess up in this school,"* waving a paddle in the air, *"we'll have a talk with this BOARD of education."*

The next morning, as he dropped Iris off at school, he said: *"Now, you go and be good, because if you don't, remember what I said." "Right,"* thought Iris.

The principal, who had been expecting her, greeted Iris at the door. *"We're going to be watching you,"* he said. Grabbing the bathing cap, she pulled the elastic strap as far back as she could and let go, hitting him in the midriff.

She turned and walked away. That was her first and last day at yet another school.

"My teenage years were so unstable. I knew my attitude and actions were wrong but I had no power to change. I couldn't turn it around. At thirteen, evangelist, Mickey Bonner, spoke at a youth night in our church. I sat at the back and somewhat listened to his sermon. As he gave an invitation my heart was racing and my hands were sweating. I remember being convicted by the Holy Spirit and thinking, *'Man, this is it!'*

After the service, Mickey and his wife, Margaret, pulled Iris aside and said: *'Iris, God made you very special but if you don't get victory over your bad attitude and complex, you're going to ruin your life.'*

"That night I ran away from home. I headed for a bar that had the reputation of letting teenagers in, and though I was only thirteen I looked very mature at 6' 3." I immediately began getting attention like I had never received before, attention from men who were three times my age, especially from one man who made a living looking for young girls and boys. He was a real freak and could spot the ones who had a bad self image, and he knew how to feed that. He manipulated me. I had never felt so important in all my life. He made me feel like I was very special. He'd brag on how gorgeous I was and I found it so easy to fall for that kind of flattery. I got suckered in. He got me an ID that said I was 22. He conned me into working in a topless bar and he was the one who turned me on to heroin and the world of crime."

The bars Iris worked in and out of for the next several years were located in the roughest part of Houston called *The Waterfront*. It stretched along the canal that ran through the area known as *The Fifth Ward* or *Bloody Fifth*. Both sides of the canal were into heavy drugs, prostitution, all the vulgar, nasty stuff, you name it. Life was cheap. Men would be found dead, murdered for just a few dollars and left in conditions that are unprintable.

"I was in prison with a girl who had killed a man for $75.00. He was in a wheelchair and she crushed his skull with an iron skillet. The judge gave her one year for each dollar she had stolen—seventy-five years."

How God preserved Iris through those years is known only to Him. Every time she was about to fall over the precipice, a hand reached out and pulled her back and it had all begun the night she resisted the Holy Spirit. God let Iris string herself out for the next fourteen years, but He did not let her go!

Where a Wrong Attitude Can Lead

They fought together. They stole together. They lived together and they got high together. They were the Bandidos. The ones Iris hung out with most were Crazy, Apple and Whitey. Whitey's real name was Winthrum Bullard, but if you had called him that he would have shot you on the spot.
He was bad!

"Preston Reynolds was the Sergeant at Arms of the *Bandidos Motor Cycle Club.4* Though I was not really his "old lady,"[5] I rode with him and lived with him. Normally, the girls who went steady with a *Bandido* were expected to wear a 'property-patch.' I wouldn't wear one. I hung out with several others but it was mostly a buddy kind of relationship. We'd sit around and play cards, gamble, do drugs—just stuff.

"When there was a fight between gangs, the 'old ladies' were never taken with them, but they took me. I was a good fighter! When I was in prison, Preston was killed. Crazy is the only one of the leaders who is still alive, as far as I know. The founder of the Bandidos, Don Chambers, died in prison of cancer. I was told that he put his faith in Jesus before he died."

Not long after Iris was saved she was watching the local Houston television news when they announced that Winthrum "Whitey" Bullard had been killed in a vacant parking lot—shot through the temple, chest and heart. The TV showed the *Bandido* parade heading for the cemetery where the members were seen throwing motorcycle parts and marijuana joints into his grave. *"I suddenly had the urge to go to them,"* recalls Iris, *"even though the burial was over—then suddenly a Scripture came to my mind: 'Let the dead bury their dead.'"*

The big one
It was a store where many of the employees of a nearby oil refinery went to cash their Friday paychecks. Iris, and three of her doper buddies had cased the place for several weeks and knew just when the armored truck would arrive to deliver the money the store would dispense later on in the day. On the way, they stopped to get gas at one of those filling stations that had several aisles of pumps with an island in the middle where you could pay an attendant. Iris knew that this station carried a good bit of money in the till at any given time, so, as one of her buddies was in the process of filling the tank, she impulsively jumped out of the car, ran up to the young man at the cash register, pulled out a knife, and demanded he hand over the money. What she didn't know was that the young man at the cash register recognized her.

Before he was able to call for help, however, they were headed for the "big one." They found a parking space near the entrance to the store and while the driver waited, the other three went inside. The armored truck arrived, and as was their habit, one of the guards carried the bag of money inside while his partner stood by the truck. Iris and her two partners watched as the store manager signed the delivery receipt and no sooner had the guard walked out, and before the manager could even head for the safe, Iris was in his face, gun in hand, demanding the money. Without so much as a word he handed over the satchel and the three ran for the get-away car. It had happened so fast that the armored car was still in sight as they exited the store.

It had gone like clockwork. They drove to where their other cars were parked, divided the loot, then scattered. Iris took her $33,000 and went straight for her parent's home. Though she had not lived there in a long time, she knew she could make a quick clothing change before heading out to start spending her take, some of it on heroin, which was one of the main reasons for the robbery.

It was now near noon when she heard someone knocking. "I was in my slip, but thinking it was my father who always ate lunch at home, I went to the door. There stood two cops and behind them a yard full of policemen, and beyond them what seemed to be a whole street full of flashing red and blue lights."

"Iris Urrey?"

"Yeah,"
"You are under arrest for armed robbery."

What on earth had happened? How did they know so quickly that she had had anything to do with that robbery? Not more than an hour had passed.

What had happened is simple to explain—there were video monitors inside and outside the store. In all her crimes, Iris never did try to conceal her identity, and now, the monitors recorded her every move. The police immediately recognized the 6' 3" female from previous arrests. Though she didn't necessarily feel invincible, Iris was uninhibited and lived with an *"I don't care what happens attitude."*

On an earlier occasion, in a robbery attempt when high on heroin, she had walked into a bar, hit a customer over the head with a glass coke bottle, expecting it to break and knock the guy out like she had seen it done on TV, but it didn't break nor knock the victim out. She turned and ran. Everyone saw her but they couldn't catch her, and this episode became just one more of the crimes she was suspected of committing, another crime that was added to the growing stack of pending warrants.

This time, however, she had crossed the line into the very serious category of "armed robbery," and after four years of suspicious criminal activity as a juvenile, they knew they had her. They headed straight for her parents' home.

Watched by curious neighbors, Iris was handcuffed, shoved into the back seat of a police car and driven straight to the county jail, a place not unfamiliar to her. She had been arrested and put in a cell on numerous occasions in this same facility, but each time her father had been able to have his teenage daughter released on his cognizance, and she was sure that he would again find a way to get her out.

But this would turn out to be different. Instead of their calling her father, she found herself being fingerprinted and standing in front of a camera for a mug shot. Then, after going through all the additional "booking" procedures, rather than being taken to a cell, she was led directly to an interrogation room.

"You have the right to remain silent. Anything you say can be used against you in a court of law. You have the right to have an attorney present during questioning, or

as in your case, being a juvenile, you have the right to have a parent or guardian present. If you cannot afford an attorney one will be appointed for you. Do you understand these rights?"

"This has never happened before," she thought. *'Where's my Daddy. I'm a minor. He'll get me out of here. He always has."* Pat Urrey was waiting outside. They brought him in.

"We know there were at least three others working with you, Miss Urrey. We want to know who they are and where we can find them."

No answer.

"Miss Urrey, if you don't cooperate it is only going to make things more difficult for you. Armed robbery is a very serious crime with serious consequences. Who were you working with?"

Iris chose the silent route, other than to look at her father to tell him that she was not guilty and that they had the wrong person. In any case, whatever the consequences, she was not going to implicate her doper buddies. Nobody was going to make her talk. As she looks back on that experience, years later, she realizes it was a pride thing. It was the kind of attitude that, four years earlier, Mickey and Margaret Bonner had warned her about.

"Iris, if you don't get victory over your bad attitude and complex you are going to ruin your life."

Now here she was, sliding faster and faster toward ruin with the attitude that no one was going to force her to do anything she didn't want to do. She was going to prove she was stronger than the authorities were. They were not going to make her confess, or snitch. She'd take the whole wrap herself.

Iris now wishes she had implicated her three accomplices. It would have been for their own good. Ending up in prison might have saved their lives. It would have protected them from themselves, as it did her. It was not long before two of them were dead, and the other one kept overdosing on LSD until he fried his brain and ended up in a mental institution for the rest of his life.

Iris soon learned that she and her three buddies had actually made another serious miscalculation in the planning of the robbery, a miscalculation that was going to affect her for years to come. As they were preparing for the heist they had considered the possibility of being arrested, and if this were to happen, they wanted to be sure their crime would be categorized a Federal offence rather than a State. This was important, because they knew how much better the Federal prison facilities were. If they ended up being caught and convicted, they at least wanted to have the best "quarters" possible.

It was for this reason they chose to rob an "armored car" delivery, which they had been told would be a Federal offence, rather than just robbing a store, which would be a State crime. What they did not know, however, is that when an armored car is involved, if the robbery itself occurs closer to the safe in the store where the money is headed, than to the armored vehicle outside, it is considered to be a State crime. This misunderstanding would ultimately determine where Iris was going to spend the next eight years.

Jail Standoff

There she sat, expecting her father to arrange her release as he had previously done on numerous occasions over the last four years.
This time, however, it wasn't going happen.

In light of the weapons charge, Iris was now considered to be a felon and a major threat to society, so the authorities decided to do all they could to keep her locked up until trial. They knew, however, that if they were to proceed with trying Iris as a 17 year old juvenile, she'd receive a substantially lesser sentence than would an adult charged with the same crime. With this in mind, they elected to ask the court to have her remanded over, without bail, until her 18th birthday. This meant nine months in the county jail, awaiting trial. The police had "had it" with this incorrigible teenage criminal. They were determined to keep her off the streets as long as they could.

To say that county and state prisons back then did not rise to the standard of the federal facilities is an understatement. Iris determined that, if they were going to keep her locked up in the Harris County jail, she was going to do all she could to make life as miserable as possible for those running the place. These next months would prove to be a standoff between one female inmate and the jailers. If they had known what they would be facing they may have had second thoughts about waiting until her eighteenth birthday to try her.

Chapters could be written about those nine months, but suffice it to say, she did her part in turning the place upside down. Fights were a daily routine. Though she didn't necessarily go around looking for them, it didn't take much to set her off. She never backed down from a good fight, and seldom was the loser. The attempts to subdue her by the jail attendants were met with the same attitude that had put her where she was in the first place. No one was going to get the best of her. They tried. They failed. Of those nine months much of her time was spent segregated from the other prisoners by putting her either in medical isolation, even though she was not sick, or in the "hole," one of the most dehumanizing punishments imaginable.

The "hole" was a 4' x 4' space with a steel door and a small window that they called a pan-hole. It could only be opened from the outside. Through this pan-hole were passed two meals a day; unseasoned grits for breakfast and unseasoned veggies for supper—never any meat. It had a high ceiling from which hung two water spickets, one to dispense very hot water and the other, cold. These were used to subdue an inmate who was unusually difficult to control. For whatever reason, Iris was never "watered."

For Iris, the most challenging thing about the "hole" was having to curl her 6' 3" body around the 4' square space that had no mat, no blanket and no pillow. It was almost impossible to sleep. Then there was that disgusting drain-hole in the floor in which she had to do everything.

The "hole" was located in the men's section of the jail, and when the male population knew Iris was "in residence" they loved to holler out to her and beat on the walls. She would reciprocate. She liked it. It helped pass the time. When the guards warned her that they were going to add one day to her sentence for every time she hit the wall, her response was, *"I hope you can count,"* as she defiantly went back to beating on the wall. The "hole" ended up being permanently closed in 1969, not long after Iris was moved to Goree. The State Board of Corrections determined it was cruel and unusual punishment.

Finally her eighteenth birthday arrived as preparations for her trial were being completed. Up to that point Iris had never admitted to her father that she was guilty, in spite of the preponderance of evidence against her. When he told her, however, what the lawyer he had hired was hoping to ask the court for, she finally confessed to the crime.

Though the State had initially planned to seek a 22 year sentence, the lawyer worked out a plea bargain with the court. Iris would plead guilty, thus foregoing a trial, in exchange for her sentence being reduced to 8 years, including the nine months she had already served in the county jail. Agreeing to this, the State would also "clean up the books" of approximately 70 other crimes she was suspected of having participated in, but for which warrants had not yet been issued. This meant that they would not be able to go back and try her on any other crimes for which, if found guilty, she would have had to serve more time. Cleaning up the books of her suspected crimes was also helpful for the justice system. It meant that there would be that much less "unfinished business" for them to deal with later.

Some "Goree" Background

"So you've been in a fight again?"
"No I always look beat up like this. What a dumb question."

In 1845, three years after Huntsville, Texas was incorporated as a city, it was chosen as the site for the State's first enclosed penitentiary. Not long after that, construction was begun on the 225 cell Huntsville Unit they called *The Walls*, and in October, 1849, a convicted horse thief became the first occupant of the partially completed facility.

In an attempt to defray costs, the state of Texas instituted what they called "inmate labor" and by 1854 there were enough convicts to justify the construction of a cotton mill adjacent to *The Walls*. Soon the mill would be grossing more than a million dollars a year through sales to the public and to the government of the *Confederate States of America*.

At the end of the Civil War, the Huntsville Unit was the only prison left standing in all the Confederate States, and with the abolition of slavery in 1865 Texas began using inmates to replace slave labor. In 1871 the state declared: *"Convicted felons forfeit their liberty and rights."* Felons were classified as "slaves of the State." Eventually this led to a *convict leasing system* under which prisoners were leased out to private interests for the building of railroads and for working on plantations. This helped alleviate the void left in the work force following abolition.

Honor, where honor is due

Following the Civil War, Captain T. J. (Thomas Jewett) Goree, who had joined the *Army of Northern Virginia* and had fought alongside General James Longstreet throughout the war, returned to Texas to take over the operations of the *Raven Hill Plantation* his mother had purchased in 1858. It would not be long, however, before Governor Richard B. Hubbard would appoint T. J. Goree to be the Superintendent of the Texas State Penitentiary in Huntsville. He served in that position for fourteen years during which time he led in many prison reforms.

A graduate of *Baylor University*, founded in 1845, T. J. Goree established weekly worship services, instituted night-class education for the inmates, and began building a library. His wife, Elizabeth, affectionately known as Tommie, became as involved in the Huntsville Unit as was her husband. She ran and taught the prison Sunday School, learned Spanish so she could personally teach the Mexican-American prisoners and, as her obituary read, attended every funeral at the prison, sometimes as the only mourner.

Not only were the Goree's involved in what they would have considered to be "a ministry to prisoners," they played a part in the establishing of *Sam Houston Institute* in 1879, and it was in their home that Governor Oran M. Roberts and Oscar Henry Cooper met to finalize plans for the *University of Texas*. And it was there, while the Goree's lived in Huntsville, that their grandson, John William Thomason, Jr. would be born—a grandson who would become known as the Marine Corps' greatest author and artist and in whose honor the navy destroyer *USS John W. Thomason* was named. It is no wonder that a unit of the Texas Department of Corrections prison in Huntsville would be named in T. J. Goree's honor.

Time changes things

In those days, less than two percent of the prison population was female, but such was not the case when Iris was driven through the prison gates. In this Goree Woman's Unit alone there were now over 700 serving time for everything from robbery to murder.

Stories have been written and rumors exchanged about *Big Iris* and her Goree years, many of which she does not remember or even believe. A fellow inmate has written a book in which she says that every time the prison staff wanted Iris to do something she didn't want to do, they would have to get *"three large strong men to handle her."* In this same book it records that *"one time Iris picked up a young 6' 2" deputy in both arms and literally threw him down the hall."* Others remember Iris as being a *"marvelous story-teller,"* while still others remember how *"she could really sing."*

There was no question that Iris spent a good bit of her time in trouble. If there was a fight, you could almost count on her being in the middle of it, often taking the side of the underdog. She did not like people taking advantage of those who were not able to hold their own. Though she may have had the reputation of being mean and always looking for a fight, more often than not, something would trigger a reaction and she would find herself in the middle of another battle which would end up with her being put in solitary. Iris picks up the story.

"Goree was segregated back then—whites with whites and blacks with blacks. Sometimes, however, when a matron or warden wanted to really punish me they would put me in an all-black *tank*.[6] Now, I have never had a prejudiced bone in my body, so that part didn't bother me. I would defend any of them as fast as I would a white girl. It would really bother me when I saw a black inmate getting punished more for the same crime a white girl committed. The matrons knew how I felt, but they also knew what kind of tension a white girl would create in an all black *tank*. So, there I would be, with hair down to my waist, washing it every night and letting it hang down to dry from the top bunk where they would usually put me.

"One time, it was just too much of a temptation for two of the girls. They pulled me from my bunk by the hair and pinned me to the floor while others began beating on me. There was no way for me to defend myself and if it wasn't for a couple other big black girls who felt that what the others were doing wasn't fair, and who pulled them off me, I know I would have been killed. It ended up in a big free-for-all, everybody beating up on everybody. The guards came running when they heard the commotion. Our *tank* was warned of this by another cell so when they arrived everyone was looking real innocent-like. But there I was, sticking out like a sore thumb—a 6' 3" white girl, covered all over with cuts and bruises.

'So, you've been in a fight again,' said the guard.
'No, I always look like this. What a dumb question."
"They didn't like my smart-alecky attitude so I ended up back in solitary."

Unlike many of the other inmates, Iris never really had a daily routine. She would "mess up," get into another fight, cuss out a matron, and end up in segregation. When she wasn't in trouble, however, you might find her sewing clothes in the garment factory, working in the kitchen, out in the yard or in the basement. The State prisons were pretty much self-supporting back then.

It hadn't taken her long to get into trouble after arriving at Goree. For one of her first punishments they sent her outside to "bust rocks." Dump trucks would drive up, loaded with big rocks which the prisoners had to break into small pieces. When Iris saw what it was doing to the hands of the girls working in the rock pile she decided that there was no way the guards were going to make her do it. She refused. About a year after Iris arrived, a prison reform act banned this kind of punishment and replaced it with shelling peanuts. That may sound a lot gentler but, as Iris recalls, it was no better.

"I've seen some girl's hands bleeding. Depending on the degree of punishment, an inmate would have to shell from one quart of peanuts up to 5 gallons. You had to squat with your back to the wall for hours while they kept bringing on the peanuts. I've seen girls crying, with their hands bleeding. I refused to do that too. They couldn't make me, though they tried. I ended up in solitary again, all by myself, to dream."

Solitary, or what was also called segregation, was often a welcome relief for Iris from the hollering, fighting, and general chaos of a "normal" prison day. It was here that she could be quiet and dream.

A place to dream
We've all dreamed. We've all escaped the "real world" to venture into a world of make-believe, taking time out to live in our fantasyland. It's a part of childhood and, for many, it's a part of adulthood. We're all the beneficiaries of master "make-believers." Without them we wouldn't have the *Chronicles of Narnia* nor the *Ring Cycle*. We would never have travelled with Gulliver nor sped across planetary space with Captain Kirk in *Starship Enterprise*. The ability of the human mind to imagine is one of God's special gifts. Inventions start with the imagination—with a dream.

But not only do we use this faculty in a creative fashion, we use it as an escape. We dream, or fantasize how we wish life would be. After WW II, hundreds of poems, written by children held in the horrible Terizin Concentration Camp[7] in Czechoslovakia, were found, expressing the children's dreams of a life that they would never know. Yet they dreamed.

Dreaming would turn out to be a very significant part of Iris' life in prison. During her eight years of incarceration she estimates that she spent at least three of them in solitary. She found this to be one of her best friends, and it was for this reason she sometimes chose to act in such a way that they would have to isolate her in order to get her under control. She welcomed being locked up by herself, with her dreams, alone in her "isolation chamber," a place that no one could invade.

"I'd dream that I was in an automobile accident and when taken to the hospital the surgeons would open me up and out would step this beautiful young thing that men would fall head over heels for. Sometimes I would dream that I was married to a husband who loved me and that we had 3 or 4 children and lived in a house with a white picket fence. Every evening my husband would come home and I would have dinner ready for him. We'd have birthday parties and we would do all those things that a happy family does. One time when I was kinda down, I dreamed about my own funeral when nobody came. There was just me, lying in an open casket, all alone."

When Iris wanted to go back to solitary she'd pick a fight, "whup up" on some inmate or do something that would upset the matron so much that back she'd go. "I'd always do this at Christmas time and most other holidays, because that way I could escape thinking about them. Even to this day, when I get down, I want to close the shades, get all alone by myself and play B. B. King music."

Never in Iris' wildest imagination did she think any of her dreams would ever come true—so she just kept dreaming.

A New Warden Arrives

"I knew all along that you were a thief, but I felt that there was something about you that was redeemable."

Clifford Olsen had never intended to be a warden. Prior to his conversion at the age of thirty-four he had had a successful international business career which, after turning his life over to the Lord, he had set aside in order to enroll in an Episcopal Seminary to prepare for the ministry. His passion was to tell others about Christ and to minister to "the least of these" in particular.

This passion eventually led to his being assigned as chaplain to incarcerated 17-21 year old men at *The Walls*, the men's prison unit in Huntsville, Texas. Unexpectedly, however, after serving in this capacity for nine years, there was a sudden turn of events that not only affected his life but that of a prisoner known as "Big Iris."

Chaplain Olsen was contacted by the director of the Texas Department of Corrections and asked to assume the warden duties at the *Goree Women's Unit* in Huntsville. A riot and fire had recently turned that unit upside down and they needed someone to take over for the Goree Warden who was retiring. They were looking for a person with a strong hand who could restructure the prison and get things under control. They felt Chaplain Olsen was the man.

Warden? This was the farthest thing from his mind. In light of God's calling on his life, to share the gospel as a chaplain, he told them he was not interested. The director, however, who was also a Christian, persisted: *"I see this position of warden as being a form of ministry as much as the chaplaincy, so why don't you pray about it for 5 days and I will pray, then we'll get back together."* After taking the matter to the Lord, Chaplain Olsen returned his call. *"I'll do it for you because I see that this position can make a statement that a Christian can run a prison."*

Iris had already served most of her sentence by the time Warden Olsen arrived in 1973. When the inmates were advised that a man would be replacing the retiring woman warden, some of them, including Iris, began looking forward to testing him. The Goree employees explained to the new warden how things operated and specifically told him who the main troublemakers were. The name "Big Iris" kept surfacing. They told him that she had an authority problem, was somewhat rebellious, expressed hostility toward the correctional officers and didn't particularly like the rules. He knew he needed to get to know her as soon as possible.

Someone who cared

"I called Big Iris into my office to have a talk with her," recalls Clifford Olsen. *"'I hope we can be friends,'* I said." Iris thought, *"Why should I want to be your friend. If the other inmates see me coming down here they're going to think I'm snitching on them."* Next night, after dinner, echoing through every cell block on every floor for all the inmates to hear; *'Big Iris to the Warden's office. Big Iris to the Warden's office.'* So down she goes.

"I want to tell you a story." Warden Olsen opens his Bible and asks, *"Have you heard about Jesus walking on the water?"* Iris recalls how he would sit there with his feet up on his desk, smoking his pipe, real casual like, reading the Bible and telling her stories.

"It was not long before I began to let down my guard. He was not talking down to me like all the others had done. He was kind of treating me more like an equal.[8] One day he said: *'I'm going to trust you enough to put you to work in the commissary.'* I thought, *'But you can't work in the commissary unless you're a trustee and I'm as far from that as a person can be.'*

The matrons were very upset when they heard what Warden Olsen had done. They told him that there was no way he should have assigned Iris to the commissary. He assured them that it would be OK. Well, Iris ended up stealing him blind. Years later, when she was able to talk with him, she told him what she had done. To her surprise, he said: *'Oh, I knew all along that you were a thief, but I felt that there was something about you that was redeemable. In spite of your reputation of being a troublemaker, you had a pleasant personality and an infectious laugh. I saw below the surface. That's why I kept inviting you to my office."*

Because Iris visited his office more than any of the other prisoners, the correctional officers became curious and the inmates began wondering what they spent so much time talking about. They of course wouldn't ask Warden Olsen, but they would ask Iris. *"What do you talk about?"* *'That's between me and him,"* Iris would say. She actually got a kick over getting the extra attention from the warden who felt God had given her to him as a special assignment.

"When I finally restructured the prison and things had settled down," recalls Warden Olsen, "I brought in David Myers, whom I trusted, and I began grooming him to take my place. I finally contacted the director with a request that I be permitted to return to my chaplaincy ministry because it was my desire to spend all my time sharing the Lord with people. He agreed. To my surprise he asked me to stay on as Chaplain at the Goree Women's Unit. That was fine with me, especially knowing that David Myers would be promoted to the head warden position. For some reason I ended up telling Iris of the change before I had advised the staff. This pleased her immensely. It led, I believe, to her trusting me even more, as I continued to witness to her until her release."

As Iris looks back on those days with Clifford Olsen, she realizes that, though she did not show any real outward change, something was happening inside. The trust and love he expressed toward her was not lost. She had always wanted to be loved unconditionally, and she felt that she was receiving this from him. Though he could have been discouraged at not seeing more evidence of God's grace in her life, he knew that God wanted him to love her right where she was. What he did not know was how significant a steppingstone this would be toward the life-changing encounter she would one day have with her Savior.

"I had always looked for acceptance," says Iris. "I wanted to be received just the way I was. I had found more acceptance from the worldly crowd I had been hanging around with than I ever did from Christians. I also looked for people who were real. I found more honesty among the folk who came to the bars than the Christians I had known in church. I know they were not all phonies, but I also knew that not many could let themselves be honest enough to really let you know how they felt or who they really were.

"The more I watched Chaplain Olsen, the more I knew he was the real thing. He didn't wear a mask. He didn't look down on me. He treated me as someone special—more like an equal.

I knew that if I ever was going to be a Christian, that was the kind I wanted to be. But I wasn't there yet."

Released

*Early release was not an option for Iris. She never earned enough points
to reach the category known as "good time," with which come certain privileges.
If she had managed to reach "good time," she could then
have worked toward becoming a "trustee."*

Becoming a "trustee" meant even more privileges, with the guarantee of early release. But Iris was not interested in changing her pattern of life in order to earn any of these benefits. When she did happen to get a few good points from time to time, it would not be long before she'd erase them by getting in a fight or cussing out a prison matron. Back she'd go to the bottom rung, back she'd go to "flat time," back she'd go to starting over from scratch.

When she was finally released, if she had given thought to living a different life style to the one she'd been living when she was arrested, it didn't last long. In spite of all Chaplain Olsen had tried to do, Iris was still convinced that what was written on her permanent Goree prison record was who she really was; *Iris Urrey—incorrigible, degenerate.* She didn't believe she could change.

Her September release was much more traumatic than her initial incarceration. When she was locked up, Iris didn't care what they did to her, but now, here she was, back on her own, in a world eight years older—a world that had changed and she had not been there to change with it. She was afraid—afraid of herself and afraid of the unknowns. And how much the world had changed began to dawn on her when she was led from her cell to the changing room and handed her civilian clothing—a pants suit to exchange for her white prison garb, and…what are these? Pantyhose?

"I looked at them," recalls Iris, "and I didn't know what to do with them. I had never seen a pair before and had never been shown how they worked. When I had been arrested eight years before, women were still wearing garter belts. I admit that it got to my emotions as I began to realize how different the world was going to be."

Dad Urrey met her at the Huntsville bus station where released prisoners were always dropped off. The prison authorities had contacted Iris' parents several days before to give them instructions as to where and when she could be picked up. Iris stepped out of the prison vehicle, this time unshackled. There stood her father who had never missed a visitation day, though often, even as it had been at the Harris County Jail, he had not been able to see her due to her having had her privileges taken away, or their having put her in solitary confinement. It was awkward for both of them, but now, at least she was free.

As Iris climbed into her father's truck the first thing she requested was that he stop somewhere for a big juicy hamburger (the kind that drips down to your elbows), french fries and a malt. She hadn't eaten anything like that in years. They stopped, she ate, then they headed back down the highway toward home. It was not long, however, before she was sick. The combination of riding in an automobile for the first time in years, and the rich food she'd eaten after eight years of prison diet, was more than her system could handle. They stopped the car, and those driving south on Interstate 45 that September morning saw a tall woman on the side of the highway, bent over, heaving, with a father, handkerchief in hand, gently rubbing the back of her neck with ice from his cup, as he softly sang to a 25 year old daughter whom he felt he scarcely knew.

> *"You're the spirit of Christmas, my star on the tree.*
> *You're the Easter Bunny to Mommy and me.*
> *You're sugar and spice and everything nice,*
> *And you're Daddy's little girl.9*

"Daddy had told me once that, though he didn't approve of my behavior, I'd always be his little girl.[10] The few letters and cards I wrote him from prison were signed, *Daddy's little girl*, though it kind of embarrassed me back then.

Home at last?
When they arrived at the house things looked pretty much the same, except for the tree out front that had grown a lot, and her nephews playing in the yard whom she did not recognize. Iris's mother was waiting at the door. She had lived in denial for all those prison years, and now, she was hoping against hope that she would be hugging a daughter who had changed. The atmosphere was understandably tense.

"Mama led me back to my old bedroom where seven[11] years of Christmas presents, seven years of birthday presents, seven years of valentine cards from the family were piled up. As I began opening the gifts, Punkin slipped me some dope when Mama wasn't looking. It was the first dope I had handled in eight years. It wasn't that I hadn't tried to get dope when I was in prison. I had almost talked Punkin into getting drugs to me when she sometimes came with Daddy to visit me in prison. Since every movement was monitored with cameras, I figured that she could pass me some pills, from her mouth to mine, when we were hugging and kissing each other goodbye. She never did go through with it, however. I guess she was afraid we might slip up and she would end up being arrested.

"Only the 'immediate' family were at the house to celebrate my release and to eat the smorgasbord Mama had prepared. Nobody had much to say during the meal. We'd never been a talkative family and we never discussed our feelings or emotions. We always had kept them hidden and I could tell nothing had changed. I could see that they would like to just forget the last eight years and get on with life. But those years in prison were not something I could easily just walk away from and say, *'I'm not going to think about that any more.'*

"Mama said she wanted me to go to my aunt's house for a family holiday. *'But listen,'* she said, *'I've told them that you've been working at the Coca Cola Bottling Company in San Antonio, so don't mention prison.' 'Mama, I'm not going to do that.'* I said. *'I hate that I was in prison but I can't just do away with all those years.'* I knew that I would mess up and talk about it at my aunt's house so I told them I wouldn't go. I found out later that while my immediate family had been lying all those years, everyone knew where I was because they had read it in the newspaper.

"Eating that first meal with the family was nerve-racking. I didn't know how to carry on a conversation or how to act. After the meal Punkin and I took off. We went to what used to be the Gulfgate Mall in SE Houston to buy clothes. I went bonkers. The styles had changed so drastically in eight years that I freaked out. I hardly knew what to buy. Punkin helped me.

"What I really was wanting most of all, however, was a good fix of heroin. Punkin helped me again. She had been a pre-teen when I went to prison and I had had a bad influence on her. Now, eight years later, though she smoked mainly pot, she knew where I could find what I was looking for, and less than 24 hours after being released, I headed back into a lifestyle worse than before I went to prison.

"I didn't go home that night."

Back Again, Sweet Heroin

"I was living dangerously, but it wasn't the exciting kind,
like being on the front line in a war zone."

You would think that after being off drugs for eight years the desire for them would be gone, or at least easy to control. For Iris, all it took was one fix of heroin and she was back to where she had been before she went to prison. But that day, after Iris left the house, she was not looking for just one fix, she was looking for an escape from the unreality of what she had just experienced with her family.

Within days, she had rented an apartment, got involved with a doper that even drug addicts were afraid of, and she let him move in with her. One morning, a month or so later, she woke up thinking: *"This is sick. I want this creep out of here,"* so she wrote him a note and left it where he would see it when he came in. *"Wayne, you've rode this horse long enough. Don't be here when I get back."* Wayne found the note, read it, couldn't figure out what she meant so he called her at work. *'I don't understand what you mean that I've rode this house long enough?''Not a house, you blankety-blank. I want you gone when I get home! Gone, you hear.'* Wayne would later kill himself.

"As a heroin addict, I was constantly thinking about my drug and how I could find money to buy it," Iris recalls. "I'd mentally check out every person I met, looking for something I could steal. Even when I had money I never knew what tomorrow would bring, so I was constantly looking for sources. I'd even read the obituary column in the local paper, bake a cake, and head for the home of the deceased during the time of the funeral. If someone happened to be home I would express my regrets, leave the cake and go on. If no one was at home, the door was often left unlocked so family and friends would be able to come and go, and I would rob them. One time, a little grandma had died and the relatives had already sorted out her jewelry and had it laying on a table for the taking. None of it was there when they returned. Nothing was beneath me."

Another source of income would be the job that was potentially waiting for Iris upon her release from Goree. She was required to find gainful employment, and through an understanding between the Prison system and Southwestern Bell, a position with them had been arranged, subject to her making it through an interview. This was part of a program that helped SWB meet the State's requirement that they hire a certain number of minorities. Iris met that criteria on two counts—she was a woman and an ex-con. When she reported to Southwestern Bell for the required interview, she pictured herself sitting behind a desk, wearing a dress and high heels, crossing her legs, drinking tea and transferring calls as an operator; *'How may I direct your call?'* They gave her a job alright, but to her shock, on her first day at work they sent her to pole-climbing school!

"I had to wear combat boots, steel-toed shoes, long sleeves, gloves and a hard-hat. I was so angry. I thought they did this because I was ugly. *'This is the same thing as the little boy in elementary school who wanted me to carry him piggyback,'* I thought. *'I'm a horse. When I think I'm going to be an operator, I end up a lineman.'* I really wanted to go and bomb their place, but because I needed a job and didn't want to go back to prison, I gave it my best shot in spite of what my co-workers thought.

"This was the time when women's lib demonstrations were on the rise and the linemen I was assigned to work with were angry that a woman was hired to do the same work that they did, at the same pay. I told them, *'Look, this is all they would hire me to do. I don't want to be here any more than you want me to be here. I'm not trying to take your job, but this is where I am. I'm sorry.'* They began to like me. I was soon partying with them."

During this period Iris was sometimes living in her own apartment, occasionally with her parents, sometimes with her little sister, Punkin, or shacking up with a guy who turned out to be married. Somehow, though staying high on heroin much of the time, she managed to keep both her daytime telephone lineman job and work the bars at night. In the middle of it all she had several more abortions, as her days and nights began running together.

"I was living dangerously," recalls Iris, "but it wasn't the exciting kind of danger. It wasn't like being on the front lines of a war zone. With all that I was involved in, life was just mundane. It was the same perverted, cheap, ungodly stuff, day after day."

A miracle moment

Three days after Iris' health insurance with Southwestern Bell took affect, she had a serious attack of appendicitis. In spite of the pain, she refused to go to the hospital, that is until her sister, Punkin, took things into her own hands and drove Iris to the emergency room. They arrived just in time. As the doctor was opening Iris up, the appendix burst right in front of him. If the insurance had not kicked in when it did, and if Punkin had not been determined to get her sister to the hospital, Iris would have just shot herself up with heroin, and died. God was protecting her, in spite of her rebellious lifestyle.

The Goree Escapee

"Punkin, two girls from Goree have just escaped. One of them has contacted me to see if I can find a place for her to hide. I can't do anything because I'm still in the hospital. I told her that you would keep her in your apartment. She should be there soon. I don't know where the other one is."

The two fugitives, one of whom was a very fine artist, had been filing away on the bars of their cell for weeks with an instrument they were able to sneak out of the workshop where, during the day, they were making jewelry. With that small file, the plaster of paris and paint they were using to make jewelry, every night they would saw away, fill the slot with plaster of paris, paint over it, then hide the shavings. Night after night they had persevered without being detected until they were able to make their escape which, according to Goree records, was the best escape there had ever been made from that facility. Miraculously, the two inmates were able to avoid the dogs in the "yard," as well as the tower guards, as they threw a couple heavy blankets over the barbed wire and gingerly dropped to the other side, and freedom. Other than a few scratches and a sprained ankle, they had made it unscathed.

Punkin dutifully did what her big sister asked her to do, in spite of her being eight months pregnant and fearful of what might happen if she were caught harboring a fugitive. She was to soon find out. In spite of Punkin's warning the girl not to make any phone calls that could be traced back to the apartment, the calls were made and, sure enough, five FBI agents arrived at the door a few days later. They were not exactly cordial, which was to be expected. They called pregnant Punkin, "fatso," as they pushed her into an armchair and began searching the apartment. The girl was easily found, but what frightened Punkin the most was what they were going to do to her, especially if they were to find the stash of marijuana she had hidden. They didn't, and after questioning her, they left.

As soon as Punkin had told her sister about the FBI visit, Iris phoned Warden David Myers at Goree.

"Warden Myers, this is 'Big Iris.' I just want you to know that I'm the one who arranged for the escaped prisoner to be hidden. I made my sister do it and if anyone is going to be punished, it's me. So it looks like you're going to get me back."

That's the last thing Warden Myers wanted to have to deal with. He neither liked nor trusted "Big Iris." He had been relieved to get her off his hands when she was finally released, so Iris believes he called the authorities off because nothing more was ever mentioned of the escape, neither by the prison or the FBI. No one knows what happened to the other escapee. She was never heard of again. Meanwhile, Iris was dismissed from the hospital, totally unaware of what God was doing.

Punkin
There was a special relationship between Iris and her "little sister," Punkin, a closeness that she did not feel with any other family members—a bond that lasts to this day. Iris was aware how Punkin had followed in her footsteps and she felt somewhat responsible for her, sometimes giving her motherly advise as to what dope she should take and what to stay away from. Iris' "counsel" even continued after she went to prison, as is seen from this brief excerpt from a prison letter she wrote after hearing that her "little sister" might be pregnant.

TEXAS DEPARTMENT OF CORRECTIONS

6-26-71
Inmate No. 209203

Dear Punkin,
    How are ya? Physically I'm fine but I've been very worried about you... You promised that you would come back this week and let me know if you were going to have a baby or not...Have you gone to a Dr. yet? I don't want you to go to one of those dumb Drs out there in the east end that I used to get dope and health cards from and...

Are you messing with acid or any other kind of dope? Weed excluded…
Punkin, don't think I've turned to a gripy old bag but I just love you and
worry about you. You know I would not even knock you for anything you
do but on the square, all things like acid, speed and stuff are bad for you
and the baby if it's there…

I really love you and I'm very worried about you but I'm with you all
the way through anything you do. We are tight sisters and nothing or even
a baby is going to break us up. So please be good for me. Bye for now. All
my love.

Stinker
(Big "Ma Ma" the badest sister in Houston)

Note: Though Punkin did sow her own wild oats, she would one day turn her life over to the Lord Jesus. She teaches Sunday School and is a grandmother who helps home-school her daughter Tara's three children—Forest, Emerald and Hunter Green.

Life goes on

Iris' bar-owner friend from earlier days had been glad to see her back. After she was released from Goree. He told her he wasn't sure how much he could trust several of the younger girls who were working for him, and knowing that Iris had "been around," asked her to help him manage his topless bars, *The Inferno* and *The Lost One*, evenings and Saturdays. This she agreed to—after all, this was her world! It was not long, however, for reasons unknown to Iris, her friend had to suddenly leave town and he turned his operation over to her. He never came back. Being a felon, she could not legally own the properties but, she did, "kind of," take over his license which she wasn't even sure was his.

She hadn't been running *The Inferno* very long before a church in the area threatened to file a lawsuit against her if she didn't take down, or change, the flashing sign over the bar entrance—a sign that consisted of burning flames with a naked girl dancing in the middle of them. They said it was offensive to their church members who walked past the bar on their way to church. Iris knew it was offensive, but she didn't much care. She wasn't about to take the sign down. Nothing came of the threat and interestingly, that church was the first church to ask her to give her testimony after she was saved.

The pastor didn't know what he would be getting into, however, when he advertised that Iris Urrey, convicted felon, *The Inferno* bar matron and former Telephone Road drugee and prostitute was going to give her testimony at the church. He began receiving threatening phone calls, warning him that if he went ahead with his plans someone was going to shoot Iris when she stood to speak. It was not until later that the pastor learned what the problem was. Iris' underworld friends thought that giving her "testimony" meant what happens in court when a witness takes the stand. They thought she was going to spill the goods on them. The pastor was rightfully scared but he decided to go ahead with the meeting anyway. When Iris heard about it, she was also scared, so she asked some of the girls from *Crossway Manor,* the ministry for girls she had just started, to go with her.

There sat Iris; convicted felon, former bar matron, with her girls around her. "*This is it,*" she thought. "*Someone is going to shoot me as soon as I get up.*" There sat the pastor, looking out over the congregation, wondering who that unknown visitor was sitting at the back. Was he going to have a murder on his hands? They all held their breath as Iris rose to speak.

But we're getting ahead of our story...

Part Two

A
New
Affection

"If you love Me, keep My commandments. He who has My commandments and keeps them, it is he who loves Me. And he who loves Me will be loved by My Father, and I will love him and manifest Myself to him" (John 14: 15, 21 NKJ).

A Sunday Surprise

"Well, I'll be. Attending church was not all that bad after all."

Iris decided it was time to spruce things up and do something special for *The Inferno* patrons. She settled on having new outfits made for her girls—bright yellow, slinky ones. She knew, at least she thought she knew, who she was going to get to make them—Aunt Bobbi.

Aunt Bobbi was not only a fine seamstress but she was also secretary to Dr. John Morgan, pastor of Sagemont Baptist Church, located not far from Iris' "business." Not surprisingly, when aunt Bobbi found out the kind of outfits Iris had in mind, and who would be wearing them, she refused to have anything to do with it. Iris, however, kept persisting, and finally offered her aunt $500.00 for the job. They settled on a compromise; she would make the dresses if Iris would promise to go to church with her the next Sunday morning. *"Fine,"* thought Iris. *"No problem. As much as I hate church I can handle one service."*

That cool, March, Sunday morning arrived, and Iris arrived, high as a kite. She'd shot herself up with heroin, but as long as she was outside in the cool air she was able to function reasonably well without drawing too much attention to her condition. The moment she sat down in the warm church sanctuary, however, she started to lose it. For the life of her, she couldn't sit up straight. She nodded all over the place and became the object of glares from those seated near her, especially from Aunt Bobbi, who began to fear what was going to happen next. Just before Iris fell completely out in the aisle, a church deacon came over, straightened her up, laid his hands on her and began to

43

pray. *"Heavenly Father…"* *"Shut up,"* shouted Iris, loud enough for half the church to hear.

This got the attention of several men from *Pulpit in the Shadows,* a Houston ministry founded by evangelist Freddie Gage. They were attending Sagemont Baptist Church that morning and in all probability they would have recognized Iris' voice as she was well known to those who were being helped by Freddie Gage and his team. They had had their run-ins with Iris, because it was not beneath her to stand outside the door of *Pulpit in the Shadows,* selling drugs to the very men the ministry was trying to reach.

One of these young men, who had been freed of his habit and who Freddie had been teaching how to witness, saw Iris as someone to practice on, someone to witness to. He went over, squatted down beside her and said: *"Can I have your phone number?"* Iris looked at him and through bleary eyes saw this good-looking dude. *"Of course, honey. You can have my phone number."* It didn't surprise her that someone in church would want her number. She wasn't surprised at all because a good many of her "clients" were Baptists. She knew that the Texas prison records showed that 78% of the inmates register "Baptist" as their religion of preference (This would vary in other parts of the country where other denominations are in the majority).

"You want my address too?" Iris was beginning to awaken from the fog. He was asking for her address so he could visit her that afternoon. *"You've got it sweetheart. Write it down. And, why don't you plan to stay for dinner?"*

"Well, I'll be," she thought as she walked into the crisp Texas March air. *"Attending church was not all that bad after all. I think I'll call some of my girls to join me. We're going to give him the time of his life. We're in for some fun."*

The Net Tightens

God works in mysterious ways, His wonders to perform!

Aunt Bobbi was discouraged. She was not holding out much hope as she left the church that morning. Her plans seemed to be falling apart. As far as she could tell Iris had not been the least impacted by the worship service. The only thing she had to cling to was what that young man seemed to be trying to do. *"God protect him!"*

Now that Iris had lived up to her side of the bargain, Aunt Bobbi knew that she was going to have to live up to her commitment and make those god-forsaken dresses. But little did she realize that, what is so often unseen to the human eye is the focus of the all-seeing eye of God who right then was drawing the net. After 12 years on the run, God was about to capture this wayward child in the net of His love. God was ready to take back this life that Satan had so mercilessly used for his purposes. God was about to shape this badly marred piece of clay into a vessel of honor for His exclusive use. Just as He had ordained it to be in eternity past, this broken, incorrigible, degenerate life was now about to be transformed into a new creation in Christ by the power of Almighty God, transformed into a vessel that would bring Him the glory it had so long sought to destroy.

Sunday afternoon: 3 PM

"Jenny, before he arrives, make sure the electric marijuana pipes are turned on and fogging up the room. Sarah, help me with the spaghetti. We're going to lace it with pot. Kelly, when he arrives, I want you to begin doing the dance that you do on the bar countertop where you slither like a snake. You'll have to do it on the floor

here. We need to decide on what music to play and make sure the light over the black velvet nude painting is on."

Roger was anxious as he approached the Winkler Street apartment. After the service that morning Freddie Gage had filled him in on who Iris was, so he knew that this was no ordinary assignment that God had handed him. All the way over in the car he had been praying and quoting scripture, and now he was about to face what would prove to be the biggest witnessing challenge he would ever encounter.

The door opened and there stood Iris, smiling from ear to ear. *"Come on in Honey."* He could already smell the familiar sweet scent of marijuana and, as he stepped through the door, he almost tripped over Kelly who was slithering across the room to the accompaniment of "appropriate" music. He knew he was entering a den of iniquity and he immediately began quoting scripture and rebuking the devil. He began walking through the apartment, placing tracts everywhere—in the microwave, in the refrigerator, on every piece of furniture there was. He even went into the bathroom where he rolled a tract up in the roll of toilet paper.

Roger did what he could to be a witness to the girls in the face of their attempts to seduce him. He claimed God's protection as he ate the spaghetti they'd prepared. He could tell it contained a special seasoning. Finally, by God's grace, he left unscathed, though a bit awed at having been in the middle of such a battle between two worlds—the evil forces of darkness on the one hand and the forces of light on the other. Iris and her girls had done everything they could to make him compromise his testimony, and they had failed.

After Roger and the girls had left, Iris went into the bathroom and when she pulled on the roll of toilet paper, out fell the tract. At first she thought it was some kind of coupon but when she picked it up, she read: *"What if it is true after all and Jesus does come back?"* Having spent her early years in church she knew what that question meant, but until now she wouldn't have given it a second thought. Then, why was the question beginning to bother her? She did her best to dismiss it.

A pursuing God

This was but the first of several contacts Roger would make with Iris over the next three days. He phoned her at the bar every night. *"Iris, Jesus loves you. He can take away your sin and make you a new person. I'm just calling to remind you that I am praying for you.*" "*Oh, shut up.*" Iris would say, as she slammed down the receiver.

Wednesday night, March 30, Roger called again: "*Iris, have you heard about the woman who had been married five times and was shacking up with someone else when she met Jesus at a well? He told her everything about herself, even things she thought nobody knew. But Jesus knew everything about her. She couldn't hide anything from Him. Iris, He knows everything about you. He sees everything you do. You can't hide anything from Him, no matter how dark it is. He sees you in the dark and He still loves you.*

Roger really got Iris' attention when he went on to say: "*Do you remember when you stood before the judge and he said: 'The State of Texas sentences you to 8 years.' Well, one day you are going to stand before THE JUDGE, not just a judge, and what if you heard him say that the penalty you were facing was death. But then, can you imagine suddenly hearing someone in the courtroom call out; 'Wait a minute. I love her so much that I will take her place.' Iris, that doesn't even skim the surface of what Jesus did for you on the cross.*"

Just before midnight, Thursday, March 31, Roger phoned again, but this time it would be a different kind of call. "*Iris, listen. Please don't hang up. I'm calling to say that I'm not going to bug you no more. No more phone calls, but I want to say goodbye to you. If you'll go outside in front of the bar I'll be there in a few minutes. I'm calling from a phone booth down the street. I'll be in my car. If you aren't outside I'm not going in. I'm not going to ruin my testimony.*"

Iris put down the receiver. What she didn't recognize, but would later understand, was that the Holy Spirit was beginning to convict her as He had 12 years before. She hadn't felt this way in all that time, now—the net was tightening.

She went to the door, oblivious to the patrons who were watching her, and stepped onto the sidewalk just as a car was pulling up to the curb. It was Roger. He opened the car door and motioned for her to get in. He was crying. "*You think that I'm not even a man because of what you and your girls are trying to get me to do. I know it would feel good but I'm more concerned about your eternity than a moment's pleasure. I've come to tell you that this is the last time I will see you. I'm not going to bug you no more. I just want to say goodbye. I'm really sorry because I know that Jesus could change you and give you everything you will ever need. But you won't let Him. You told me once that you used to dream about being a lady. Well, I guess it's only going to be a dream. I'm not going to hang around with tramps. I'm not going to hang around you and ruin my life. You just don't understand that Jesus can take an old tramp and make a lady out of her."*

Iris recalls: "When Roger said that word, *LADY*, it was like someone hit me in the pit of the stomach with their fist. I had daydreamed so often about being a lady when I was in solitary confinement. More than anything else that's what I wanted to be, but I never thought I could. Now, Roger is telling me that... He was still crying.

"I thought, '*but I'm a junkie. If I become a Christian, can I be a Christian junkie? I'm shacking up with two guys right now. Can I just shack up with one and let the other go?*' I knew in my heart what the answer was. I knew I had to let go my past. I looked at Roger and through my own tears I said; '*I want to be a lady.*'

"He wiped his eyes and said: "*OK. If you mean business, if you really mean what you say, you'll get out of this car and kneel down right there on the sidewalk in front of your bar and ask God to forgive you. Kneel down right there on the sidewalk. I'll go with you.*"

"We got out of the car and walked to the middle of the sidewalk in front of *The Inferno*. Roger took my hands, but before we knelt down he said: '*This is going to be kinda like a wedding when a minister leads a couple in their vows. It's not just believing in Jesus that saves you because if it was, you would have been saved the first time you heard the truth. It's a commitment of your life to Him. By faith you say, 'I give you me.' But like in a marriage, it's not a one way street because when Jesus gets all of you, you get all of Him.*

"We knelt down on the sidewalk. One of my girls was dancing in the window of *The Inferno*. The music was so loud I could feel the vibration on the sidewalk, and they were not playing, *Just as I Am*."

Roger: "*Are you ready?*"
"*I am.*"
Roger looked up and said: '*Jesus do you want Iris?*'
I waited for a moment, then said: "*I don't hear anything.*"
Roger: "*Jesus said, 'I DO.' In fact, He already said 'I DO' to you 2000 years ago on the cross.*"
"*OK, Iris; do you take Jesus?*"
"*I DO.*"
Roger: "*You know she ain't worth anything...*"

"*Woah!*" I thought.

Then he said: "*But Jesus you bankrupted heaven for her.*

"*Now Iris, is there anything you are not willing to give to Jesus?*"

"I remember saying, *I'll be willing to sleep in a ditch for the rest of my life if you really will forgive me and take away my yesterdays and make me a lady.*"

The girl in the window was no longer dancing. The music was no longer playing. It seemed as though no one else was around, except Iris, Roger, and God.

Just a few steps were all she had had to take, and not unlike Naaman, who had to dip seven times in the Jordan to be cleansed of his leprosy, that day, Iris Urrey, the incorrigible degenerate, **knelt down a tramp and stood up a lady.** The net had been drawn. She had been washed clean of the leprosy of sin. The transaction was completed. She was a new creation. The angels in heaven sang.

Roger and Iris went back to the car. They talked about what it meant to be a Christian and what it was going to mean to Iris' future. It was now 2 AM, Friday. Suddenly Iris said: "*Roger, I remember that they always sang a song at church when people got saved. I can't remember what it was. I think it was something like 'Take me as I am.' Isn't there supposed to be music when people get saved?*"

At that, Iris began singing the only song she knew that came anywhere close to what she remembered was sung in church—the Burger King theme song, "*Have it your way at Burger King. Have it your way, have it your way!*"

Iris never returned to her topless bars. She never went back to the apartment where she'd been shacking up. To this day she doesn't know what happened to her furniture, clothes or jewelry. She doesn't have to. Though it is not unusual for dopers and prostitutes to lose their possessions many times over, this time she didn't give it a second thought.

Lady Iris would never look back.

"I DO"

"It's not how bad we've been, it's how good Jesus is!"—Iris

R-i-n-g…R-i-n-g…

"Hello…"

"Roger, I'm not sure I'm saved. I don't feel anything."

"Iris, do you normally call people at 3 o'clock in he morning, doubting your salvation?"

"No."

"Then, can't you see that you are already different?"

CLICK.

Fifteen minutes later. *"Roger, how can I know for sure that I'm saved?"*

"Iris, I'm tired. Let me get some sleep. I'll talk to you tomorrow."

CLICK

Iris must have doubted her salvation a hundred times in the next two days as she struggled with how God could really change her from the tramp she had been to the lady she had always wanted to be. It really was more shock than doubt. The change was more traumatic than anything she had ever experienced and she was struggling with how to handle it. Though she wanted to tell her sister, Punkin, right away, she didn't tell her what had happened until she went to her apartment on Saturday.

Punkin wasn't home, so she waited, trying to process her thoughts and emotions. When her sister finally returned with little Tara, the baby Iris adored, Punkin looked at her and said, *'What's wrong with Aunt Stinker?'* She knew that something was different.

"I got saved, Punkin."
"Well, don't preach at me."
"I won't.

Iris picked little Tara up and began studying her tiny hands. She looked at them in a way she had never done before. For the first time she noticed the delicate veins and the little fingers. It was as though she had a new pair of eyes. She remembered how she had blown marijuana into that precious face just a few days before, and how she had tried to teach little Tara to say bad words. Now it was beginning to hit her how different everything seemed to be. She was coming out of shock.

Another sign that things were changing was how anxious Iris was to go to church the next morning. She could hardly wait. She had hated church for most of her life, and the only time she had gone to a service in 12 years had been the week before, and what a stir that had caused.

Sunday morning
"I arrived early and headed straight for the front row. The Lord knew exactly what I needed to hear. The pastor spoke on God's forgiveness. He read Psalm 103:12, *'As far as the east is from the west so far hath He removed our transgressions from us.'*

"'*Oh, sir, I ain't educated but I now know that even I can't get there from here,*' I called out from the front row. Now, preachers don't like you talking back to them when they're preaching, so he moved to the other side of the platform and began talking about a man named Nicodemus who came to Jesus at night. *'I did too,'* I said out loud. *'I came to Jesus Thursday night.'* He then read John 3:6. *'That which is born of the flesh is flesh but that which is born of the Spirit is spirit.'*

"All of a sudden it was like God was pulling a curtain back from my heart. I began to understand why He had saved me. I began to even see how He was going to use me. I began to understand what my personal testimony was going to be, a testimony that I have shared around the world, that around midnight on March 31, 1976, out in front of an old bar in Houston, Texas, I knelt down a tramp, a loser, a zero, but stood up a lady. When I stood up I was clean, pure, forgiven, innocent, blameless, cherished by God and brand new.

Salvation explained

"A lot of people know about Jesus, but I got to know Him personally when a young man explained to me that it was like a marriage. Salvation is like you receiving Jesus and Him receiving you. But it starts when the Holy Spirit begins convicting you of your need of Jesus and telling you what He'll do for you. People explain the experience in different ways. Some have a sensation of guilt, some of a growing hunger to know God, some experience confusion over whether there really is a God and what He could do for them; whether He could really change them. But, whatever the revelation or sensation is, it can come only when the Holy Spirit is doing His work of drawing you to Jesus—creating a desire in you to know Him.

"I believe the Holy Spirit uses the testimony of what God has done in my life to create a hunger in others. That may be happening in your life even as you are reading this book. You may be wondering if you too can really be forgiven and have your yesterdays, the things that you wish you could forget, taken away. For me, one of the greatest things about my salvation is knowing that my yesterdays are gone, that the blood of Jesus has washed them away.

"When that happens, He gives you a peace for each day. I'm not afraid of yesterday or tomorrow because I have peace for today and hope for tomorrow. I used to have to daydream because I didn't have any hope for the future. There are a lot of people who are like that. They have no real hope so they have to fantasize or dream of what they wish they could be. Is that where you find yourself? Are you wishing you could experience a change in your life that will make you a new person and give you hope? Do you want God to change you?

"A lot of people don't go any farther than saying they love Jesus. They have never committed themselves, or turned their lives over to Him. That's why I like the illustration of it being like a marriage. People hear stories about Jesus and are told that they need to love Him. My Daddy used to compare this to having a crush on somebody, flirting with someone, but not being willing to commit to marriage. That's the way it had been with him for many years before he finally said '*I do*' to Jesus. You can shack up with someone, and even have children, but that doesn't make you married. What makes you married is when you believe it in your heart, then you stand in front of witnesses and say, '*I do!*' That's another way of saying what the Bible says in Romans 10:10. '*For with the heart man believeth unto righteousness; and with the mouth confession is made unto salvation.*' You believe it, you know that this is what you want to do, then you get up and say, '*I do.*'

"I'm going to ask you to do something here that I have asked thousands of people around the world to do. I'm going to ask you to join me in an *'I do'* prayer. If you feel that the Holy Spirit is speaking to you, convicting you of your need of turning your life over to Jesus, and you are ready to do that, I invite you to make this your prayer. Or you may prefer to just use this as a guide and use your own words. It doesn't matter.

Dear Heavenly Father,
I confess that I am a sinner and that I deserve death and hell. But you loved me
so much that you sent Jesus, your only Son, to die in my place. Though I don't
understand it all, I receive Jesus as my Savior, as the payment in full for all my
*sin—past, present and future. I say, "**I DO**" to Him and I turn all that I am over*
to Him and receive all that He is for me. Thank you for forgiving my sin; thank
you for making me clean; thank you for making me a new person. AMEN.

The Journey is Launched

You don't have to go far to find someone in need;
You don't have to go far to sow the Gospel seed;
You don't have to go far, just start right where you are,
You don't have to go far to tell the story.12

Iris was walking on air when she left the church that morning. It had been less than three days since she had said *'I DO"* to Jesus on the sidewalk in front of *The Inferno*. How could things be so different?

She had skipped work at the telephone company on Friday, the day after the Thursday encounter. She found herself so "high," but this time not on drugs, that she just couldn't let down long enough to return to her lineman work. Now that it was Monday morning, however, she knew she needed to report if she expected to keep her job, and keeping it now was more important than ever, because the thief, drug addict and bar matron had died.

She was anxious about how she was going to act, or what she would say. She knew her conduct and language was going to be different and she wondered how her fellow workers would respond. As she walked into the assignment room the boss called out: *"Hey, Iris. You're supposed to be 'cross town at the pot-wiping class."* (This was a class where you were taught how to wrap telephone cables with lead). Iris' initial response showed that her sanctification was barely underway. She was about to say: *"Kiss my foot. I just got saved,"* but she didn't.

Iris remembers the *pot-wiping* class that was held in a yard next to the pole-climbing school.

"As I looked over at the poles I started to cry. What used to look like a telephone pole now looked like a cross to me. The teachers of the *pot-wiping* class had us pair off, two to a board, each with a seat on either side. I was so nervous I hardly said a word to my partner all morning. I wasn't sure how I should walk, how I should talk—I was so afraid of messing up.

"During lunch break I sat in my car reading the Bible, praying and crying. When I got back to my board after lunch, I heard my partner on the other side singing a hymn, one that everybody and their dog knows—one I remembered hearing in church years before. I was so excited. I whispered to him: *'Hey, I just got saved.'* He then got all excited and started giving me advise, encouraging me and praising the Lord. All week long he continued to talk to me: *'If you have an uneasy feeling about something, or if people put pressure on you to do something you don't feel right about, stop. Don't do it. That's a caution light warning you. Rule your life by that caution light and you'll have the peace of God.*

"'Be careful when people try to sway you by making you feel sorry for them. That's what dopers do. When you hold up a godly standard, it makes them feel guilty. If they can get you to compromise to their lower standards they don't feel so bad.'"

Iris continues to follow his advise to this day. She is aware that God placed him in her life as her *pot-wiping* partner for her first week as a Believer. She needed someone to encourage and instruct her.

After work each night, Iris went back down to the area of Houston where she had felt most at home over the years, but this time it was not to a bar, it was to the Christian drug rehab ministry, *Pulpit in the Shadows*. She was well known around there because she used to sell drugs behind the building to the guys they were trying to help. This reputation ended up being a problem after she was saved. Iris had been attending the evening chapel services for about a week when Freddie Gage, who had been away on a trip, returned. When he saw Iris sitting in the front row he shouted:

"What are you doing here?"
"I got saved," Iris replied.
"Get out of here," he ordered.

It was too much for Freddie to believe that God could change her. He just knew she was up to no good. Iris started to cry as she got up to leave. *"My old friends don't like me because I talk about Jesus, and those I want to be my new friends don't like me because I have old friends. I don't know where to go."*

This was but one of the minor setbacks Iris would experience as she adjusted to her new life. A few days later she began witnessing to the line crew. They were not quite sure how to handle this "new" Iris so they decided to check her out. She was in the office one day, copying a Bible study, when one of the guys asked her to join them for a beer after work. This was not unusual as she had done everything with them in the past.

'I didn't really want to go', remembers Iris, "but I had not yet learned how to say, 'NO.' Besides, I had been a doper, not a drinker. I didn't even like alcohol. When I hesitated he said; *'What's wrong? You mean Jesus would be mad at you for just going to have a beer with your friends?'* I hesitated, then gave in. I thought, *'It's not going to hurt to go with them for one beer.'*

"The moment I said I would, I knew I was doing wrong, but I went anyway. As we sat in that bar I began to cry. *'Guys, I'm sorry. I shouldn't be here.'* I began telling them why I no longer belonged in a place like that. I shared what had happened to me. They never asked me again.

"When I left the bar I went straight back to the drug rehab center. Though I had had only one beer you would have thought I'd been drunk for 6 weeks. I was feeling so guilty. When I confessed what I had done to the guys at the center they said: *'Just don't do it no more.'*

"Just don't do it no more?' Fine. But how do I know I will be strong enough to not do it the next time? It was then I decided that I was going to have to start burning bridges that connected me to my past. I had heard about Christians doing real good for a while, then messing up, and that terrified me. Now this may not be the way other new Believers would think of burning bridges but I figured that if I offended the people I used to run with, they would not want to be around me, and the way I would do that was to keep talking about Jesus to them. Those who wanted to get saved would stick with me and the rest would not.

"What I called burning bridges others call witnessing. I rode up and down the road where I used to hang out, burning bridges, one by one. I went into bars, the Dairy Queen, Western Auto, the pool halls, the bikers' club and the ice-houses. I'd say: '*You're not going to believe what happened to me. Honey, I was garbage. I might not know how to act like a Christian yet, but I know that Jesus is real. He changed my life and forgave me. I'm pure, clean, forgiven and blameless.*'"

When Iris got to the Dairy Queen she headed straight for the little walk-up window where she usually placed her order. They all knew her there. She stuck her head in the window and began telling her story. The cook, standing behind the half-wall in the back hollered. "*Can I meet Jesus?*" Iris almost knocked her head off as she raised up. "*I don't know. I guess so. Let me make a phone call.*"

She went to the pay phone and called her pastor. "*What do I do? This guy wants to get saved.*" The pastor asked her to see if the cook could take a short break. The manager agreed to it and in a few minutes Iris and the cook were crammed into a "Superman-type" phone booth, and as Iris held the receiver, the pastor, the cook, and Iris held a three-way conversation.

Pastor: "*Tell him the Bible says that we all are sinners, every one of us. It says that, all have sinned and come short of the glory of God.*"
Iris: "*Honey, did you know that the Bible says that we are all sinners, every one of us?*"
Pastor: "*Tell him that the wages of sin is death but the gift of God is eternal life.*"
She repeated it.

They went through the whole plan of salvation and then they prayed.
Pastor: "*Dear Heavenly Father.*"
Iris: "*Dear Heavenly Father.*"
The cook: "*Dear Heavenly Father.*"
Pastor: "*I know I'm a sinner.*"
"*I know I'm a sinner,*" Iris repeated.
"*I know I'm a sinner,*" echoed the cook.

This was the first time Iris had prayed with anyone to get saved. She was thrilled that God would let her be a part of it. She knew that she personally could not save any one but was learning how God was going to allow her to participate in His reaching the lost. She was overwhelmed as she began to see people being transformed from the kingdom of darkness into the Kingdom of Light.

Witness training

Not long after this experience with the cook, Iris attended a soul-winning class called the *WIN School,* similar to *Evangelism Explosion.* The classes ran Sunday night through Friday night, then, on Saturday, they went out witnessing. This was so new and exciting for Iris. The desire of her heart was to be as well equipped as she could be for God's calling on her life.

"One night toward the end of the week," she recalls, "we were asked to share our testimony in just 60 seconds. *'Sixty seconds?* I thought. *'What in the world can I say in 60 seconds?*

"*'OK',* the teacher said. *'Here's how we're going to do it. Everyone count off, one, two, one, two, etc. Then, all the 'ones' turn around to the 'twos' and I'll give you 60 seconds to give your testimony. Then the 'twos' will take their turn.'* We counted off and I ended up a *two* standing next to a little old lady who was a *one.*

"She turned slowly toward me and in a sweet soft voice said: *'Oh, I was raised in a Christian home and I've never really gone out in the world...'* As she was finishing her testimony I was thinking, *'60 seconds to tell where I've been and what has happened to me?'*

"*'Now twos, it's your turn.'* I looked at that sweet, gentle, lady and blurted out; *'Honey, I've been a whore, I lived on drugs for years and I'm an ex-con.'* My little partner stopped breathing for a moment and almost fell over."

That's the Truth!

"When He, the Spirit of truth has come, He will guide you into all truth…He will glorify me, and He will take of what is mine and declare it to you" (John 16: 13a, 14a).

Houston evangelist, Mickey Bonner, was part way through his message when he suddenly stopped. Sitting there in the congregation was the girl he had warned, fourteen years before, that if she didn't get victory over her bad attitude and complex she was going to ruin her life. He couldn't believe his eyes. He had never forgotten that night and had prayed for her over the years, especially after hearing that she had ended up in prison. But now, here she was, in church, beaming from ear to ear.

Mickey couldn't help himself. He shouted: *"Let the redeemed of the Lord say so. Is there anyone here who has just met Jesus and would like to share what He has done in their life?"*

Iris was so engrossed in taking sermon notes that she had no idea he was asking her to give her testimony. After a few seconds an elderly lady stood up and in tears said: *"I think it's me. I need to share my testimony. I went to buy groceries today,"* she said between sobs, *"and they put the eggs right on top of the sack. The young boy who helped me to my car didn't close the door well and when I turned the corner the door opened and the bag fell out. There were twelve eggs in the sack but only one broke. It reminded me of the disciples when only one out of twelve turned bad."* Iris thought, *"What on earth is she talking about? I don't know nothin' about cracked eggs but I have a testimony!"* With that she jumped to her feet and shared what God had done in her life. It was a time to celebrate.

Mickey took Iris under his wing, providing wise counsel and guidance for this young believer. Sometime later he invited her to his ministry's Board of Director's banquet where a man by the name of Manley Beasley would be speaking. This proved to be a divine appointment of the first order. Iris' life would never be the same again. For the first time she heard what it really meant to walk by faith.

This is it!

"It thrilled me," Iris remembers. "When I got saved I had sensed that not only was I now headed for heaven but that the way I would live from then on would be completely different because I had become a new person. I knew that when I lived in the world and worked in the world, I thought and operated the way it did, but now that I was saved I didn't expect to ever live like that anymore. Though I was very young in the Lord I just knew that God was going to be my source of supply, not only for some things, but for everything."

With this conviction, Iris began to look at other believers to see how they lived this different kind of life. What she saw, however, were people depending on the same things the world depended on. She heard preachers on TV begging for money. She saw churches planning budgets the same way businesses in the world did. She saw very few people whose lives could not be explained in human terms, but now, here was someone talking about faith that went beyond saving faith for salvation but a faith that touches every area of life. Manley Beasley was even saying that without this kind of faith it was impossible to please God. Iris could hardly believe what she was hearing. *"This is it,"* she thought. *"What this preacher is saying is what I've been looking for."* She had the witness of this truth in her heart, but she had never heard it explained the way Manley was now explaining it. She knew she was hearing truth and she knew that this was the kind of life she wanted to live.

"When the banquet was over," Iris recalls, "I ran up to Bro. Manley and blurted out: *"I'm a converted whore and an ex-con and I've got to know more about what you said tonight."* Bro. Manley started laughing. *"You need to call my wife,"* he said. Without thinking, Iris, still not long from the streets, shot back, *"Why, was she a whore too?"* *"Well, no,"* replied Manley, *"but I think you two will hit it off."* He gave Iris their home phone number and it was not long before she and Marthé were "hitting it off," and it was not long before both

Manley and Marthé knew that God had entrusted to them this unrefined, young, tramp-become-lady for His divine purposes and glory. This was but the beginning of a relationship in which God would use the Beasley family to shape this former heroin addict, woman of the street, thief and ex-con into one of His beautiful trophies of grace. None of their lives would ever be quite the same again.

Two weeks later, Marthé invited Iris to join them at First Baptist Church in Euless, Texas for a *Deeper Life Conference* where Jimmy Draper, the church's pastor, Jack Taylor, Ron Dunn, Dr. Culpepper, Miss Bertha Smith, Dudley Hall and Manley would be speaking. Iris didn't know what a *Deeper Life Conference* was and the only speaker she had heard of was Bro. Manley, but that didn't matter. She was ready to go. *"We're going to fly you up here from Houston and you can stay with a lady friend of ours,"* Marthé told her. Iris was excited. It would be the first time she had flown from Houston to Dallas. Everything was set, that is until the night before she was to leave. The phone rang. It was Harley, one of her old *Bandido Motorcycle Club* buddies. He was crying. *'Iris, everything has happened. I can't even die.'*

Months before she had witnessed to Harley at an Ice House on Telephone Road, in Houston, where he and his biker buddies were drinking. *"Have y'all heard what happened to me?"* she'd asked them. *"Guys, we were all wrong. The way you are living is not what life is all about."* Harley, half drunk, stepped up behind her and poured beer all over her head. *"Now,"* he said, *"when you go to church they'll smell the beer and will kick you out because you have to be a teetotaler to go to church."* He kept cutting up until Iris got so mad she pushed him up against the wall. *"You punk,"* she said. *"You're going to listen to me."*

"That was the last time I had seen him or heard from him until this phone call. He was really broken up as he told me his unbelievable story. As a result of a motorcycle accident years before he had had a steel plate put in his leg. On his new job, while painting a billboard with a roller, he had hit a high voltage wire. The shock had thrown him thirty feet and the electricity had blown the plate right out of his leg, but that is what saved his life.

"While he was in the hospital he had developed a rare and very contagious virus of the bowels. They put him in isolation which meant he couldn't have any visitors. There he was, leg in the air, bowel virus, no visitors and his wife didn't even phone him. When he was finally released from the hospital no one was there to pick him up. When he finally got home there was nothing left in the house. Everything was gone except for a 38 snub-nose revolver—no refrigerator, furniture, nothing but a note from his wife saying that she had left him. That was all he could stand. He took the revolver, pointed it at his heart and pulled the trigger. Somehow, the bullet missed every vital organ, but it tore him up so badly that he ended up back in the hospital. They patched him up. Now he was home, wondering why he had not died.

"I had just finished reading the whole Bible and remembered how it says in Revelation 9:6, when the fifth angel blows the trumpet during the tribulation, that men would seek death but would not be able to find it. Being the great theologian that I was, I knew immediately what was happening. *'Oh, my God, Harley. You can't die. We must be in the tribulation. Harley, you can't get saved. It's too late. You are going to hell. I'm so sorry,'* I sobbed. By then Harley was freaking out.

"A few minutes later Bro. Manley called to discuss the trip I was to make the next day and to ask me if I would share my testimony at the conference. *'I don't know,'* I sobbed. *"What's wrong, sister?'* he asked. *'Oh, Bro. Manley, my friend just told me... I just realized...we're living in the tribulation and he can't get saved!'* Bro. Manley started to laugh. I thought, *'What's so funny. Harley is going to hell.' 'Call him back,'* Bro. Manley said. *'Tell him we're not in the tribulation. Now you need to get some things straight. Since Harley called you it means that Jesus is calling him. He is under conviction. Tell him that we are not in the tribulation and that he can get saved.'*

'I called Harley. *'Guess what I just heard. I made a slight error. The truth is that we are not living in the tribulation and what is really happening is that Jesus wants to save you. Come over right away. I'm having a Bible study with some friends and I'll tell you how.'* Ten minutes later. *Bam, bam, bam!* I opened the door and Harley fell to his knees. 'SAVE ME!' he cried.

"I phoned Marthé. I told her about Harley and asked if it would be all right for him to come with me to Euless? *'Sure,'* she said. *'We'll find a place for him to stay.'* So, the next day Harley, the saved Bandido and I, flew on Southwest Airlines to the *Deeper Life Conference.*

"On the plane I told Harley that I didn't know exactly what this conference was about but that at the end of the church service the speaker would explain the way of salvation and would invite people to go to the front to pray to be saved. *'You've already done that.'* I said, *'but you still need to go forward when he asks people to respond.' 'OK,'* said Harley.

"When we arrived at that first service we caused a bit of a stir. There I was, all 6' 3' of me, being led around like a pet bear by Marthé, as Bro. Manley described it, with Harley following along behind, dressed in his Bandido outfit—bright colorful vest, chains, motorcycle boots, the whole thing. People were looking at us like, '*What are they doing here?*'

Ron Dunn preached that morning. No invitation. We sat there listening to speaker after speaker, all day long, and none of them gave an invitation. Finally, the last speaker that night was Bro. Manley. When he finished he gave an invitation. As Patricia Owens walked toward the piano, he said, '*No music. If it takes music to get them, it will take music to keep them. If you want to do business with God, if God has dealt with you about anything, then come now.*'

"The center aisle of the church had pews in the half round. Fifteen rows back the pews in the middle zigzagged. It was a beautiful sanctuary for a wedding but weird for walking forward at an invitation. Harley couldn't figure out how to get over to the aisle from his pew but that didn't stop him. He couldn't stand it any longer. He jumped up and took the straightest line to the altar which was stepping from the back of one pew to the other. Nothing was going to stop him from getting to the front. The congregation was shocked, but that didn't bother Harley, and it didn't bother Bro. Manley either. He knew what was happening. God was all over that place that night. Harley, the Bandido, was home!

Iris stayed in touch with Harley for several years. He returned to the Houston area where he became part of a church fellowship. He married a Christian girl and as far as Iris knows, he is still going on with the Lord.

Lessons to Learn

"Teach me your way, O Lord, that I may walk in your truth; unite my heart to fear your name" (Psalm 86:11). ESV

Learning the walk of faith

It must have felt like she was lying on her back at the foot of a waterfall with her mouth wide open. The amount of truth Iris was taking in at the *Deeper Life Conference* was almost overwhelming, and added to the sessions at the church were the between-times she spent at the Beasley house, sitting at Bro. Manley's feet.

"He would tell me Bible stories," Iris recalls. "He talked to me just like I was a little child. I was hearing things about being a Christian that I had never heard before. I began to understand what walking by faith really meant. I knew that this was the life I wanted to live. I soon learned, however, that it was not going to be easy but, with Bro. Manley's and Marthé's help, I was determined to learn it and walk it.

"I admit that there were times when I would get really frustrated with Bro. Manley. He watched me struggle to believe God for certain things, like going to the *International Congress on Revival* in Europe. He told me that I was going to have to trust God for the money. He would ask me, *'Iris, are you going to the Congress?'* I would say, *'I hope so.'* He would say, *'Well, you're not going because it's going to take a lot more than hope to get you there.'* I would get mad. He told me years later how in those early days of my learning to walk by faith that he had wanted to help me out financially, but he knew that if I was going to grow, my faith had to be tried and tested. To the glory of God,

I never missed any of the *International Congresses on Revival* and I have seen God work miracles in so many other situations over the years."

From the moment Iris heard Bro. Manley explain the walk of faith, she became totally committed to making it her life, and some of the lessons she learned came at the most unexpected moments.

A lesson in the sky

In Iris' *Prelude*, at the beginning of this book, she tells of the lesson on faith she learned as she sought God's financial provision that would enable her to travel with Manley Beasley and a ministry team to Alaska. The faith miracle did not stop with the long handles, pink bows and finances, however. God had another lesson awaiting this young believer on the airplane.

They had not been flying long before Bro. Manley introduced Iris to Ed Greig, one of his closest friends. A few minutes later, Ed sat down beside her to say that God had shown him that she was to witness to a certain stewardess. This initially turned Iris off, as she thought, *"If God wants me to witness to that stewardess He can show me Himself."* Ed then turned to the row behind them, where several of the team members were sitting, and said: *"God just told me that before the plane lands in Anchorage I'm going to have an extra $200.00 to spend, above and beyond what I brought with me."* Iris thought, *"Well, I bet if I said that loud enough for everyone on the plane to hear I could come up with $200.00"*

About that time the co-pilot walked by, and as he did he stopped, looked at Ed, and almost shouted, *"Ed Greig, what in the world are you doing on this airplane? I thought you and your wife were ministering in Mexico."* *"We are,"* said Ed, *"but the Lord has opened a door for me to go with Bro. Beasley to preach in Alaska and that's why I'm here."* The pilot then reaches for his billfold, pulls out a check and says: *"I've been carrying this $200.00 check around with me for weeks, waiting to find out how I could get it to you."*

Iris sat there with her mouth wide open as the pilot continued. *"I wasn't supposed to be on this flight but I had to step in at the last moment to take the place of another pilot who had to cancel due to an emergency."* All of a sudden, while the pilot was still talking, the stewardess Ed had told Iris she was supposed to witness to came down the aisle and sat beside her. *"What are y'all going to be doing in Alaska?"* she asked. Iris thought, *"Did Ed send her back to me?"* She knew better. He hadn't. It was God who had spoken to Ed Greig. It was God who was now placing this young stewardess next to Iris, and it was God who opened her heart to the message of Jesus' saving grace. And the angels sang...!

Learning to be a lady

In addition to learning about the life of faith, Iris had a lot to learn about being a lady, due to the rough life she had lived in and out of prison. There was no question in her mind that God had changed her from a tramp to a lady on the inside that night on the sidewalk in front of *The Inferno* bar in Houston, but now, she wanted to be like a lady on the outside as well. She wanted to learn how to act and look like the lady she had dreamed of being during those many times in solitary confinement.

Not long after she had been saved, Iris had begun wondering how a Christian girl should dress, so she asked her pastor. *"Stand in front of a full length mirror and take a good look, then ask yourself if you would be embarrassed if Jesus returned right then,"* he said. She got the message and went from one extreme to the other. She went from suggestive looking clothing to wearing long dresses with long sleeves and high collars.

One night she showed up at Punkin's apartment dressed in her "born again" attire. Four of her acquaintances were smoking pot with her sister and they tried to get her to join the circle where they were passing joints from one to the other, in both directions. When she refused, they started making fun of her. One of them said, *"What have they done to you?"* To her shock, James, Punkin's degenerate husband, defended her. *"Shut up,"* he said. *"Can't you tell she's different now!"*

Remembering how Christian girls used to dress back in those days, compared to how they dress now, Iris wonders what has happened. "Some of them dress the way I used to dress before I was saved, when I worked the bars on Telephone Road in Houston," remarks Iris. "I really don't understand it.

"I knew I had so much to learn, and I knew that I wanted first of all to please Jesus, so not long after Marthé Beasley and I had become friends, I phoned her. *'Marthé, I've lived like a tramp for so many years that I don't know how to act like a lady. I've been praying for someone to teach me and God has told me you are the one.'"* Marthé picks up the story,

Dining etiquette 101

"What Iris said was pretty straight and to the point so I decided we would begin with dining etiquette. I took her to the Southern Plantation, one of the nicest restaurants in Dallas, for her first lesson in table manners. Bro. Manley, Ron and Kaye Dunn and a few others were with us. The waiters and waitresses dressed with ruffles at the neck, wore those stockings half way up their legs, and had towels hanging over their arms. The food was fabulous and the place really did look like a Southern Plantation.

"'OK, Iris, listen to me. When I say, ladies never do that, mark it down in your head. We must never forget that Christian ladies should be more proper than anyone else because we represent Jesus. We're the King's children. Now, here's the first lesson. After you have been seated at the table, take your napkin and put it in your lap. Then, put your left hand in your lap. Understand?'

'Marthé, can I say something?' Iris interrupted.

"'No you may not. You have asked me to teach you to be a lady so you sit there quietly and listen. Now, with your left hand still in your lap, take the fork in your right hand and take a bite of the food. Then, lay your fork down on your plate, get your roll and take a bite of it. Then, put it down, chew what you have in your mouth then start over again.'

'Marthé, can I say something now?' Iris asked me again.
'Yes, what is it?'
'I'm left-handed.'

"I took a deep breath. 'Alright, Iris, put you right hand in your lap and just do the opposite of what I've told you. And don't forget to keep your right hand in your lap at all times.'

"Before long Iris was talking away and I noticed that that she had both elbows on the table, with a roll in one hand and a fork in the other, swinging both of them as she was telling me something important.

"'Ladies NEVER do that,' I grunted, as I smacked her hand. I hit her hand so hard that the roll flew over three tables and landed in a man's lap. I stared at Iris. 'If you dare turn around to see where that roll went, I'll get up and walk out of here and never speak to you again. Just keep eating and, GET YOUR ELBOWS OFF THE TABLE.'"

A Testimony

Herb Peavy

President of *The Horizon Foundation*, Atlanta, GA,
and treasurer of Iris' ministry board in the 1980's

*"I know I do a lot of things wrong, but if I'm going to miss God I'd rather miss
running toward Him than running away from Him"—Iris*

"There are many stories that I could tell about Iris Blue that would be unbelievable yet all would be true. Many would be extremely funny, some sad, but all would depict a most unusual person and a wonderful miracle of our God. I will not attempt to recall all of these stories but simply share one that was a tremendous witness to me and one that was used to stretch me to yet another level in my Christian walk of faith.

"I met Iris in 1982 when she was introduced to me by a dear friend who had met her at the *International Congress on Revival* in Europe. Because of her powerful testimony and ability to minister to people from all walks of life, we decided to move her to the Conyers, Ga. area where we would be in a position to better help her develop her ministry. We went through the legal process of creating her ministry with a board of directors and all the other bells and whistles that it took for this entity to be a genuine ongoing ministry. This was 8 years after I had rededicated my life to Christ and was bound by a Christian "hard work ethic" that caused me to be blind to the understanding of 1 Corinthians 13, the love Chapter.

"Early on in my relationship with Iris I recognized a uniqueness about her that I loved, but at the same time confused me tremendously. One of my responsibilities as a board member was to help her with the financial end of the ministry. I soon realized that I would not just be "helping" with this chore but, because she had no interest in the financial end of things, I would be handling all of it. It would not be long before I became quite vexed with her because she would not spend time learning about paying bills on time nor work at holding down expenses, such as selecting the least costly airline tickets.

"Although I was the ministry treasurer, Iris had the authority to write checks. This became a big problem because she was constantly writing checks to people who needed help. This was becoming a problem, especially to me, because it made it more difficult to make ministry plans since we never knew how much money we were going to have in the ministry account. This caused a strain between Iris and me to the point that, upon hearing us argue about it, an unknowing soul would assume we had both lost our salvation, if we had ever been saved at all. These disagreements drove Iris to tears more than a few times, after which I would feel awful.

"As frustrating as this was, however, I was observing things in her walk that amazed me. She understood and practiced a genuine love of all people. She looked past a person's "warts" and accepted them as they were. She understood true forgiveness. As soon as she realized she had offended someone by loosing her temper, or anything else that came even close to sinning, she would immediately repent. I began to see that her walk with our Lord was a much deeper one than mine, and this began to cause me much anguish. I was a deacon in my church. I was a Sunday School Teacher and an avid tither yet, I saw a freedom in Iris that I did not have.

"The "stretch" for me began when Iris went to speak in a rural church in South Georgia. While there someone told her of a family who had just lost everything they owned when their house burned. Iris got to visit with these folk and she was deeply moved by their situation. Meanwhile, back in Atlanta, we were thanking God that we had gotten the finances together to send her to Germany for three months to work in the European Baptist Convention churches under leadership of Bob Ferguson and the Faith Baptist Church in Kaiserslautern. We had managed to accumulate $5300.00 for this project. Iris returned from South Georgia on Monday and I met with her that evening to discuss her upcoming trip. You can imagine how horrified I was when she told me that she had given $5,000 to this needy family out of the funds we had in the trip account. I have long since been ashamed of what I said and the manner in which I said it. It ended with Iris crying, even though she was still convinced that she had followed the will of God in doing what she had done. At the time, I thought it to be the most irresponsible action I had ever witnessed. We barely spoke for a week.

A short time later, Dr. Charles Stanley, Pastor of First Baptist Church of Atlanta, invited Iris to speak at his early Sunday morning service. My wife Vicki and I drove her to the church and as soon as we got there we learned that Dr. Stanley was suffering from severe back problems and would not be able to preach at the second service. That being the case, Iris was asked to do that service as well. Although I was genuinely sorry for Dr. Stanley, I was thinking this must be of the Lord since there would be a love offering taken for Iris at both services, rather than from only the early one. This, I knew, would help us recover at least some of the money she had so "unwisely" given away. At the first service the sanctuary was nearly full and many people, moved by Iris' testimony came down to talk with her at the end. There was only one problem. No one thought of taking up a love offering!

I was irritated to say the least. My only consolation was that I knew the second service would have an even larger crowd, so at least we would get the love offering from that one. The second service turned out to be more powerful than the first. As Iris shared her testimony you could hear people weeping all over the sanctuary. A large number of people responded to the invitation at the end of the service. It was wonderful to see how God was working, except for one thing—no one thought to take up a love offering.

I was furious. How could this happen twice? After most of the people had left the sanctuary, Tommy Gilmore, Dr. Stanley's assistant, walked up to me and apologized for not thinking of the love offering. He said that both services were so powerful that the love offering was just simply forgotten about. I tried to act spiritual and said something about how God had always provided for Iris and I felt sure He would continue to do so. Tommy then told me that Dr. Stanley had requested her to speak again that night and that he, Tommy, would make certain a love offering was taken. I remember thinking, *'Yes, and at a Sunday night service, even at this great church, there won't be enough money in the love offering to buy her enough gas to get her home.'* Tommy told me that once the offering was counted he would cut a check and I could come by Monday to pick it up. I was hoping for maybe $800.00. I didn't even attend the service that night.

On Monday I drove the few blocks from my office to First Baptist Church, had a cordial conversation with Tommy Gilmore, picked up the check and left. Once in my car, I opened the envelope and found the check to be for a little over $4,800. I was astounded! With this and the money that had surprisingly come in the previous week we now had more than enough to replace the $5,000 Iris had given to that needy family.

I went back to my office but did not call Iris for several hours. I was having to process a lot of things. Was Iris really as unwise as I had thought her to be? Was she really following the will of God when she gave the $5,000 to that family? Was my conservative "business man common sense" approach to finances the best way to be a good steward of what God had provided? Although I had not yet settled on answers to these questions, I finally called

Iris to let her know the good news about the love offering. She was not the least bit surprised. Before the conversation ended, however, I could not help telling her that we needed to discuss her giving away things on a whim, before she did it again. I will never forget her response.

"I know I do a lot of things wrong but if I am going to miss God, I'd rather miss running toward Him than running away from Him."

Now I was the one doing the weeping, right there in my office. I wasn't weeping about my salvation—that had been settled years ago. I was weeping about my not yielding to God on a daily basis and letting the little foxes slip into the vineyard and steel away my "dying to self," which is not a one time event but a daily "must". I began to realize that I had adapted a spirit of religiosity that was a poor substitute for a genuine walk with Christ. Iris knew this all along, but never accused me of it. She just loved me anyway and prayed for me until her prayers were answered. I thank God for the strong, true and deep friendship that we continue to have, and I thank Him for the impact her love and friendship still have on my life to this day.

The Invasion Continues

*"But you shall receive power when the Holy Spirit has come upon you;
and you shall be witnesses to Me in Jerusalem, and in all
Judea and Samaria, and to the end of the earth" (Acts 1:8).*

It would soon be clear that God's plan for Iris' life and ministry would be uniquely shaped to who she now was and from where she had come. The years that the locusts had eaten, years spent in the kingdom of darkness, would now be used to invade that kingdom with the glorious light of the gospel. And invade it she did.

Very soon after the *WIN* training, Iris shared her testimony with a girl who had turned her house into a massage parlor. As is true in many of these businesses, the massage service really was a front for other activities such as sex and drugs. When the young lady turned her life over to the Lord she closed down the operation and returned to her home state. In appreciation for what God had done in her life through Iris, she decided to give Iris her property; lock, stock and barrel, which included all the debts.

Crossway Manor
Iris saw this as an open door from God to begin a ministry to abused women, drug addicts, lesbians and prostitutes. She fixed the house up, changed it from a massage parlor to a message parlor, and named the place, *Crossway Manor*. Isaiah 54:2 was the scripture God quickened to Iris' heart for the girl's home.

"Enlarge the place of thy tent, and let them stretch forth the curtains of thine habitations; spare not; lengthen thy cords, and strengthen thy stakes."

The police, who were astounded at the change in this person who had once been categorized as an incorrigible, began bringing some of the "first offender" girls they were arresting, to *Crossway Manor*. Usually, these were young girls picked up for prostitution or first time marijuana possession.

It was not long before a nearby church became aware of what Iris was doing and offered their help. This eventually resulted in their giving her the use of a vacant house adjacent to the church parking lot. The original "message parlor" house was sold and the *Crossway Manor* ministry moved location. Not all the church members, however, were pleased with this arrangement as they were suspicious of Iris' ex-con credentials. Because of this the pastor felt he should not put Iris on the church staff but agreed to let her work as a volunteer. This didn't matter one way or the other to Iris, all she wanted was freedom to minister to her girls.

Iris recalls: "Here we were, me and my girls, now located next to a church. Word was getting out among the "underground" about what I was doing at Crossway Manor and what the police were doing to help some of the first time offenders. One day a black stretch limousine pulls up. I knew immediately that it meant trouble. These were members of a crime syndicate that ran one of Houston's prostitution rings.

" *'Go get the pastor,'* I ordered one of my girls as I peaked through the window. *'Hurry!' The rest of y'all go! Go'!* They all snuck out the back door and ran to the church. I was left by myself staring at the limousine. I don't know how long it was, but it seemed at least 30 minutes went by. They didn't roll down the window or honk the horn. I admit I was scared. My heart was racing. *'Where's the pastor? Perhaps he's calling the cops.'*

"When I could stand it no longer I walked out to the car and just stood there until they rolled the driver's side window down. *'What do you want?'* I asked, trying not to show that I was shaking. The guy in the passenger side said: *'We want our girl back.'* I knew who they were talking about.

"Do you know what we are doing here?" I asked.
"I don't care what you are doing here. I can kill all of you." He was cussing up a storm.
"My knees were getting weak but I was trying to be brave.
'I can't let her go with you. She doesn't want to go.'

'What is she doing here?' he asked.

"'This is a Christian home. I am an ex-con, drug addict, prostitute and I spent 8 years in prison, but I got saved. My life has been changed. Now, I try to get girls off of drugs and out of prostitution. That's why your girl is here. She wants to get off of drugs. She's been going to church with me.'

'Did she get saved?'
'Not yet, but I believe she will. She doesn't want to leave here. She's memorizing Bible verses.' That set him off to cussing again.

'All right, I'll make a deal with you. I'll let her stay. But if she ever goes back on the street she's dead. We'll kill her.'
'That's a deal,' I said. *'I'm going to make sure that she won't run to anyone but Jesus.'*

'You're crazy.' He said as he began to cuss again. *'No, I'm not,'* I said, *'and I've got the papers to prove it.'*
'Give me your phone number.' 'No, I can't do that,' I said. *'I'm not going to let you talk to her. You can call me, but not her.'* I gave him the church's phone number. He wrote it down and drove off.

Iris went straight to the pastor's house and rang the doorbell. He answered. *"Do you know where the girls are?"* she asked. *"No,"* he said. *"I've been standing on the toilet looking out the bathroom window to see what was going on. I knew you were safe. I was doing warfare praying for you."*

The next morning Iris and the church staff were sitting in the church office discussing what had happened the day before when the pastor's secretary came in to say that Iris had a phone call. It was the syndicate guy.

"Yo, Iris. I'm back up here and I've been thinking about what you are doing. I just want you to know that if there is anything you need, and I mean anything girl, just let me know."
"You mean that if I want somebody killed you're telling me I can call you!"
"I didn't say it that way. I just said if you need anything."

"These guys had really scared me but God had protected me and my girls. But I confess that I was really mad at the pastor for hiding in the bathroom, even though he said he was praying."

The miracle of Mary Jane

"Remember what Bro. Manley said? 'You can't unscramble a scrambled egg.'"

The Pasadena, Texas, police stopped to check on the female hitchhiker. When asked who she was and where she was going, she responded in unintelligible gibberish. She had no identity on her. Aware that they were dealing with someone with mental problems, they decided to take her to *Crossway Manor* rather than put her in a jail cell. They knew she would be safe with Iris until they determined who the woman was.

"I've never worked with retards before. I've got a house full of prostitutes and drug addicts. What am I going to do with her?"
"Just keep her for a few days until we get this sorted out. Do whatever you can. We don't want to put her in a cell with someone who might hurt her."

Mary Jane had escaped earlier that morning from the Austin, Texas Sanatorium and knew enough to try to make her way back to where her mother lived. Years before, her single mother, not knowing how to handle a mentally ill daughter while trying to make a living, had had her daughter, who was now 32 years old, committed to the Austin facility. Now, here the daughter was, in God's providence, being placed into Iris' hands.

"What's your name?"
"Mary Jane."
"Well, Mary Jane, if you stay with us you're going to have to keep our rules. One of them is that every day you have to memorize a scripture if you expect to eat. We're going to be eating supper in a little while so here's a verse and when you've memorized it you'll get to eat."
"I can't. I'm retarded."
"If you can tell me that you're retarded, you can memorize a scripture verse."

"Mary Jane threw a fit," recalls Iris. "She cried, she screamed, so I put her in a bedroom by herself, gave her the verse on a piece of paper, and told her that when she learned it she could eat. I don't remember how long it was, probably 2-3 hours, before she came out."

"I can, I can...do...all...things...through Christ...which strengtheneth me" (Philippians 4:13).
"Well, praise the Lord! See, you can do it!"

The next day Mary Jane memorized another verse, then another, then another, day after day she was memorizing along with all the other girls.

As they waited word on what was going to happen next, Iris began to sense that God had a larger purpose in bringing Mary Jane to her, larger than just providing temporary care, so she contacted several of her board members to see what they thought about her attempting to get legal custody. Two of the members, one a city councilman, and the other, head of the Pasadena Water Department, offered to contact a Judge they knew who might take the case, and it was not long before documents were prepared and a time set to meet in the Judge's chambers.

In the meantime, Iris had taken the girls to hear Manley Beasley who was in a nearby meeting. Manley spoke on *The Danger of Believing a Lie*, using the illustration of Jacob believing, for years, the lie that his son Joseph was dead. Manley gave an invitation that night and Mary Jane was the first to respond. At the altar, she told Iris and Bro. Manley that all her life she had been told that she would never be able to do anything because she was a retard. *"I believed what they said, but it was a lie. I'm not retarded, I can memorize scripture verses."* That night, 32 year old Mary Jane was set free!

As the time approached for them to appear before the judge, Iris received an unexpected phone call from an agency that had been assigned to take Mary Jane into custody. They said that they would be picking her up in an hour and taking her to Houston's *Herman Hospital* where she would be kept until the court hearing. They advised Iris not to say anything to Mary Jane about their coming because the records showed that she was a "rabbit," someone who would try to escape and run away. Iris was not about to mislead Mary Jane, however, so she sat her down and explained what was going to happen.

"Listen carefully, Mary Jane, and don't get upset. Some people are coming to get you and they say that when they do that you will try to run from them. Now, here's what I want you to do. Go and brew some fresh coffee and when they come, you answer the door and say: 'Hi, won't you come in and have a cup of coffee.' You serve them and when they ask you to go with them, do what they say. They'll take you in a car to a hospital not far from here where you will stay until we all go and talk to the judge. It won't be very long before we will come and get you. I promise. OK?"

And so, the time to appear before the Judge arrived. Iris, Mary Jane, her mother, the city councilman and the head of the Pasadena Water Department sat watching the Judge as he read through the documents. Finally he looked up. *"Mary Jane cannot function in society. She has been in a mental institution for most of her life..."* Before he had finished the sentence, Mary Jane, who had taught herself that, every time someone said *"cannot"* to immediately quote the first scripture verse she had ever learned. When the Judge said, *"she cannot function..."* Mary Jane stood to her feet:

"I can do all things through Christ which strengtheneth me. Philippians 4:13."
"You hush," said the Judge. *"You're to speak only when I ask you to."*
"A soft answer turneth away wrath, but grievous words stir up anger, Proverbs 15:1," was Mary Jane's reply.

The Judge looked stunned. Iris and the city councilman exchanged glances. For a moment the world stood still. Iris, though not wanting to offend the Judge, but feeling someone needed to say something, said: *"Your honor, a lot of people have lived in society and have never memorized a scripture verse."*

God turned the heart of a Judge. Iris, the 28 year-old ex-con was awarded custody of 32 year-old Mary Jane who began calling Iris, Mom. Sometimes, when out shopping, Iris would hear, *"Mom, look at this."* Mary Jane loved Iris. She was constantly looking for ways she could serve her "new mother." One time, when Iris had gone to the bathroom in the middle of the night, she returned to find that Mary Jane had made up her bed. When Iris had to correct her, or discipline her for doing something wrong, her reply always was: *"Remember what Bro. Manley said, 'You can't unscramble a scrambled egg.'"*

The rest of the story is just as beautiful. Mary Jane's mother, who saw what was happening in her daughter's life, began visiting her at the Manor. Iris had explained to Mary Jane that what her mother had done was what she had felt was best for her daughter and that she had meant no harm. Mary Jane began to reach out to her mother in love. She told her mother that she forgave her for what she had done and it was not long before her mother had turned her life over to Jesus.

Mother and daughter would soon be legally reunited and it would not be long before the mother, with Mary Jane as her helper, would start a small office cleaning business. Their first contract was cleaning the Pasadena mayor's office.

Iris stayed in contact with them for some time, even after she had moved to Phoenix. The last she heard was that the office cleaning business had grown, that additional personnel had been added, and that mother and daughter were doing well.

In search of a lost sheep

Some time later, a group from the church was scheduled to go to a *Bill Gothard Seminar* to be held at UCLA, in Los Angeles, California. Iris and Marthé Beasley were going with them and the night before they were to leave Iris got a phone call from Shirley, one of her girls who had run away from Crossway Manor a couple months before.

"I'm in California and I want to come back. I'm in a commune and they won't let me leave because I owe them money for living here. Can you help me?"
"Where in California are you?"
"Los Angeles."
"OK. We can handle that. We're heading for Los Angeles tomorrow. We'll be there in two days. Give me your address and phone number. I'll call you when we get out there."

Iris remembers how all the way from Texas to California the pastor talked about rescuing this girl. When they arrived at the hotel the staff was all a-dither. Elvis Presley had just died, but for Iris, thinking about Elvis' death could wait, she had a mission to accomplish. She phoned Shirley to get directions, and soon, the pastor, Iris, Marthé Beasley and the driver were on their way.

As they pulled into the commune the driver, a bit anxious at what he saw, turned the Greyhound bus around and had it ready for a quick exit. As Iris and Marthé were stepping down from the bus, the pastor told them that he felt it best that he stay behind on the bus to do warfare praying.

"I now know how important warfare praying is, but back then I thought the pastor was really afraid and was using prayer as an excuse not to go with me. He may have been, but, whatever, we were there to rescue Shirley, so, with Marthé following me, I got out and walked toward the main building. The door opened and before I could say anything, this guy was in my face: '*I wrestle alligators.*' he said.

Having the background Iris had, she knew right away that this was just a scare tactic, and he could tell he hadn't scared her. He probably had not met many woman as big as Iris. *"Really?"* she said. *"Do you want to wrestle with me?"* That took him by surprise, then to his amazement, the older blonde woman (Marthé) spoke up:

"Why are you staring at my ear like that. I don't appreciate men staring at my ear."

"I'm not staring at your ear," he said.

"Yes you are. Look at you. I know it looks strange. I have this cauliflower ear because I was a wrestler in College and it left me looking like this. Go ahead and touch it. I know you want to. Go ahead."

"This woman is crazy," he thought.

"Oh, go ahead and touch her ear," Iris said.

The alligator wrestler could never have anticipated what would happen next. As he reached out to touch Marthé's ear she showed her teeth, snarled like a mad dog and pretended to bite his arm. *"He must have jumped three feet in the air,"* recalls Iris.

It did not take him long to turn Shirley over to them, and as he watched the three walk back to the bus, he realized that his plan to get money out of them had gone awash. This was the first time he had failed to not only scare someone, he had failed to scare two women! *"And, what was that blonde talking about? Her ear looked perfectly normal."*

The pastor watched through the rear window of the bus. The sheep had been rescued.

A Trial of Faith

*"Now faith is the substance of things hoped for,
the evidence of things not seen" (Hebrews 11:1).*

When Iris established the *Crossway Manor* ministry she did so with the conviction that she was to trust God for His provision and, not unlike her mentor, Manley Beasley, she determined not to go the route of fund raising appeals—she would take her needs to the Lord and look to Him to provide all that was needed to carry on the work. Though this went against the wishes of her board, made up primarily of deacons from the church that was making the ministry house available to her, she felt she could not compromise her convictions.

"I hear a lot of people talking about the walk of faith," Iris says, "but I don't find all that many who really practice it because, as I have found in my own life, it is a lot easier to talk about faith than it is to practice it. There have been times in my own walk that I have gotten in the flesh and would start worrying about tomorrow, especially when faced with serious financial challenges. All I know to do then is to confess it to the Lord and go back to trusting Him with my tomorrows.

"God put me in a school of faith early on when I was running the girl's ministry at *Crossway Manor*. I had continued working for the Houston Telephone Company after I was saved but found it was like working two jobs—the Girl's Home and the phone company. There just wasn't enough

80

time in a day for both so I decided to quit climbing poles and begin trusting God to meet all our needs.

My board of directors, however, who were godly men, were wanting me to run *Crossway Manor* more like you run a business than by faith. They wanted me to send out appeal letters and have fund raising events, but I didn't believe that this was the way God would have me go. I didn't want it to look like I was begging for money. My mind went back to those years I spent in bars. I remember the drunks laughing and ridiculing TV evangelists. *'Hey, there's another one whose God is big enough to grow an arm and a leg but He's not big enough to pay the light bill.'*

"One of my board members asked: *'What if you end up with no food for all those girls?'*
"Well," I said, *"I'll just have to tell them, 'Honey, I guess God's not as big as we thought He was, so go back on the street and hustle.'*

"I had learned that, even in bars, people will be generous to someone who really has a need, like when a cripple or a homeless person walks in and says, *'Man, can you help me? I don't have anything to buy food with.'* They'll pass the hat. They're not heartless, but they're not godly either. I saw a difference between doing something for someone when you feel sorry for them, and giving to the Lord's work because you feel He is leading you to do it."

There were times when Iris had as little as $5.00 to feed ten women. She'd take the girls to the store where they'd buy green beans, potatoes and pinto beans. That $5.00 would go a long way. It became an adventure for all of them.

Iris had had very little experience in paying bills so, when she had the responsibility of doing this for *Crossway Manor,* she made a few mistakes. When the water bill arrived that first month, and it was for only $10.00, she decided that since it was so small she'd wait until the next month's bill and pay them both at the same time. When those two bills only came to $20.00, she decided to wait for the third bill. What she didn't notice on the third month's bill was the fine red print that said they were going to cut off the water if she didn't pay the whole amount immediately.

When the Utility person arrived she was told that, in addition to the $30.00 back payment, she was going to have to come up with a $60.00 deposit to have the water turned back on. She didn't have $90.00 to her name. She looked around and couldn't see anything she could hock. One of the girls teasingly said: *"Why don't you call your board of directors?"* *"No way,"* Iris said. *"They'll just want me to send out a newsletter!"*

What was she to do? They had to have water. *"Girls, while I go over to the gas station to get the key to the restroom, you all get your Bibles and starting in Genesis, look for all the places where the word WATER is used."* The girls began finding water everywhere; *no water, part water, bitter water, sweet water, water coming out of rocks*…they found all kinds of water references. This kept them busy while Iris was praying about what her next step would be.

While she was praying, one of the girls went into the bathroom. She screamed: *"There's a stream of water coming out of the bathtub faucet."* They ran to see, and sure enough, there was a little stream of water running into the tub. They checked all the other faucets—no water. Only in the tub! When Iris returned she had them scrub the tub then she showed them that when they plugged the drain they didn't have to worry about it running over, because of the emergency drain near the top. *"The tub will stay full to that level,"* she said. *"You can dip your glass in it to drink, we can brush our teeth with it, we can cook with it, use it to flush the toilet; we have water! You may not see this as a miracle, but I do."*

One of the girls sitting on the side of the tub, and who had just been reading her Bible, spoke up. *"Hey, it says here that if I drink this water I'll thirst again, but if I drink the water Jesus has, I'll never be thirsty again,"* "We talked about the living water Jesus gives," Iris recalls, "and right there in the bathroom we led her to the Lord. God gave us another miracle."

"I could have gone to any church or bar in town to tell what was happening to these girls who were trying to get off drugs, and they all would have given us the money. I could have even collected $90.00 at a four-way stop, but God wanted us to experience a miracle. *'God, I'd rather drink this miracle-water out of this tub for the rest of my life than go and beg for money.'*

"A few days later a man who had a business just down the road stopped by to chat about the work we were doing with the girls. His name was Virgil Weekly and he owned the Cimarron Paving Company. When he asked for coffee I simply grabbed a pot without explaining anything to him, walked into the bathroom, filled it with water, came back and made the coffee. I didn't say a word about our water being turned off.

"After we visited a while, he left, but it wasn't very long before his wife, who was also his secretary, was knocking at the door. *'My husband has asked me to tell you to send him your water bill, light bill and phone bill.'* I got so excited thinking that he was going to pay all those bills for the month, but I didn't know half of what God had told him to do. He had the billing addresses changed over to his address and I never did see another bill. He paid them all, right up until the time we closed the ministry down. If I had gone asking people for the $90.00, I probably would have had to do that every month.

From famine to feast
"I remember the time we were completely out of food. The cupboard was bare. Not a thing to eat. All I had left was one dime. *I could phone my sister, Punkin,'* I thought. *I know she would bring us some groceries.'* But I also knew that the girls would hear the *plink, plink* of the dime dropping into the phone, and anyway, I really wanted more than a sympathy gift, I wanted the girls to see something that could not be explained. I prayed; *'Oh God, please show us a miracle.'*

"That very day a man came to our door with cases and cases of *Wolf Brand Chili.* Now, Texans think that Wolf Brand is the best chili in the universe, but no matter, if we didn't have anything else, we did have chili. *'Hallelujah,'* I'd sing. *'We're having fried chili today.'* On another day I'd announce: *'Glory to God. We're having roast chili today!'* We had chili for breakfast, chili for lunch, chili for dinner; we had chili for three straight days!

"At the beginning of every meal we would always take each other's hand and sing the little chorus, *'This is my commandment that you love one another, that your joy may be full.'* When we finished singing I would pray, *'Thank you, Lord, for your provisions and bless our meal time. Amen.'* On the 3rd chili day, when we sat down to breakfast, Carla, one of my girls, got so mad that we were having chili again she started spitting out the words to the song. She knew that if she didn't at least join in, no matter how she felt, that I would make the girls start the chorus over from the beginning and keep singing until everyone participated, and she didn't want to do that.

"When we had finished the chorus she blurted out: *'If God is so blankety-blank good, you tell him that I want some blankety-blank bacon and eggs for breakfast tomorrow morning. I'm sick of this stuff.'* I was so embarrassed. I just knew that God was going to strike her with lightening . As I stormed out of the room, I huffed, *'I don't want to be in this room when God gets you.'* I was so mad at her.

At 7 o'clock the next morning a woman banged on our door. She had brought eleven sacks of groceries. She said, *'I'm leaving town on vacation and the Lord told me to go ahead and buy all the groceries our family would normally use in a week and give them to you.'* Sitting on the very top of the first sack were the *blankety-blank* bacon and eggs. I cooked them, made grits, biscuits and gravy, and sausage. We had a smorgasbord of food in front of us.

After we had sung our song, I looked at Carla and said: *'Carla, honey, you started this and I know I got very upset, but apparently God listened to you. I wouldn't have. I would've struck you with lightening. But He's a lot better God than I would ever be. He honored your request so why don't you thank Him for our breakfast this morning?'* We bowed our heads and waited, and we waited. Finally Carla could only get one word out. She whispered, *'God!'*

"I could have made phone calls, sent out a newsletter, and God may have provided for us that way. But that's not how He has called me to trust Him. As it happened, Carla saw God's hand that morning. Later on in the day, one of the girls shared the gospel with her and for the first time since she had come to stay at the home, she was ready to listen.

'Carla, they told me that I could be forgiven and meet Jesus by admitting that I was a sinner. I did that and I invited Him into my heart. That was just a few days ago and I really feel different. You can do that too.' Before the day was out, that new young convert, from off the streets of Houston, had led Carla to the Lord. I didn't. I was too spiritual. I was still mad at her for cussing.

"I wish I could tell you that all the girls turned to Jesus. They didn't, but I never judged the success of the home on the number of girls who got saved, I judged it on the lessons and truths God was able to teach us. He really did care for us. If we needed to be stretched financially it was because God was wanting to do something in our lives that money couldn't do. He always knew what we needed."

Crisis at Crossway Manor

"Follow peace with all men, and holiness, without which no man shall see the Lord: Looking diligently…lest any root of bitterness springing up trouble you, and thereby many be defiled" (Hebrews 12:14-15).

When Iris returned to Houston from California she discovered a growing resistance on the part of more and more of the congregation to the *Crossway Manor* ministry. One of the issues had to do with her girls attending the services. It was making some of the church members uneasy. The way the girls looked, and the way some of them acted, was disturbing. Many members began questioning whether or not they should even be allowed to attend church. Iris recalls how the services were beginning to look like a segregated congregation—all the "bad" people sitting on one side and all the "good" people sitting on the other. In retrospect, Iris now better understands what the church was going through.

"As I look back through the eyes of a mother," she now says, "I can understand how they must have felt having homosexuals sitting there with their long eyelashes, bandido bikers in their leathers and chains, and girls not exactly dressed like Sunday morning worshipers. Some of the members were even afraid of going to the rest room in case some of my queers and prostitutes were in there. It must have been tough on them, but all I wanted to do was lead these kinds of folk to the Lord and I was naïve enough to think that all Christians would be excited to see sinners, right off the street, attending church, no matter what they looked like. I thought that this way it would be clear to them who they needed to pray for."

The pastor, in an attempt to bring some kind of order to the conflict, suggested that Iris form a Sunday School class for *wayward women*. This would provide a place for "Iris' girls," while keeping them separated from the rest of the youth. This did not go over well with Iris who wanted her girls to be a part of the church community and not feel segregated. She wanted so badly for them to find Jesus, and have them feel accepted by Christians, that she reacted to this suggestion and ended up not handling it as well as she might have, She had not yet learned the niceties of church vocabulary or protocol.

"What do you want me to do?" was her response to this suggestion. *"You want me to stand in front of the church and call out, 'All you whores, come on in. We've got a special Sunday School class just for you.'"*

Not being able to really understand the passion Iris had for her girls, and not knowing how they could make the adjustments Iris wanted them to make, it was not long before the church leaders called her in to say that they were putting out a fleece to see if they were going to be able to continue having her ministry connected to the church. She didn't know exactly what putting out a fleece meant, and she didn't know what they were looking for. All they told her was that if God allowed a certain thing to happen then they would know that they would have to ask her to leave.

Whatever they were looking for must have happened, because it was not long before Iris had no option but to begin closing *Crossway Manor* down. An irony in it all was that—though the church wanted her to take all the "bad people" with her when she left—contrary to their wishes, a number of them chose to continue attending the services because they liked the pastor.

This was a very disillusioning experience for this young zealous, Christian. It led to her having to deal with a resentful and bitter spirit. She didn't know how to cope with what she interpreted as rejection of both her and her ministry. "It broke my heart. I wanted to die. I wish I could say that I left the girl's home in victory, but I didn't. I was bombed out. *'Man, nobody wants me,'* I thought. I was sick."

Fortunately, or better put, providentially, the Lord had brought Manley Beasley into Iris' life. He was becoming her spiritual father and mentor. When she was facing difficulties he was the one she would call for counsel. They had talked a lot about what was happening between *Crossway Manor* and the church, and now she needed him more than ever as she dealt with bitterness. God led Manley to, in his unique way, lead Iris through her crisis. She remembers it well.

"Bro. Manley would say: *'Iris, do you have the victory?'* I'd say, *'Yes, but... they've ripped my heart out.'* He'd say, *'Victory doesn't have a but.'* I'd get mad. *'What do you mean victory doesn't have a but? Bro. Manley, they're making me close the girl's home. They say they are going to turn it into a crisis pregnancy center and the man who has been helping pay my bills is going to pay them and I'm not going to be anywhere around.'*

"Bro. Manley would say: *'Iris, you have to choose to forgive that pastor. You can't hold a grudge. It's a choice. You choose to forgive those who offend you. If it just lasts for 10 minutes and you get mad again, choose to forgive him again. Next time if you last 30 minutes, choose to forgive him again. You keep choosing to forgive until one day you aren't bitter any more.*"

"*'I'm not bitter,'* I would say to myself. But I knew I was. Bro. Manley would call me again. *'Iris, do you have the victory?'* I'd say, *'Yes, and I'm not going to say, but.'* I'd try to word it another way and he'd say, *'You're not there yet.'*

"One day he asked, *'What are some of the prayers you have been praying? What are you asking God for?'* I thought about that and God began to show me my heart. *'Well,'* I said: *'I've asked Him to strike them with a bolt of lightening; to just singe the hair off of a few of them, but it looks like He just blesses them.'*

"So, you're even mad at God?'
"I didn't say that.'
"You don't have to say it that way.'

"Bro. Manley knew I was mad and bitter, and I knew it too. I would tell God that I forgave them and I would ask God to bless them, then I would wake up the next morning and be mad all over again."

Though she had done nothing wrong at the girl's home, rumors were spreading. *"I've heard that she was letting those girls do stuff. They're saying that..."* And on and on it went. This eventually led to most of her speaking engagements being cancelled. She began to receive calls from churches expressing their regret that, due to some kind of conflict, their plans had to be changed. What really hurt in all of this was that no one asked her to explain what had happened. Iris is not sure that that would have even mattered all that much, as it would have been the word of an ex-con against the rumors of more "mature" Christians.

But during all of this, God was watching. There was still a lot of shaping to be done in the life of this young "saint" and it was going to take a while, but, as the song that Iris would eventually sing, says:

> *He's changing me, my blessed Savior,*
> *I'm not the same person that I used to be.*
> *Well, it's been slow goin' but there's a knowin'*
> *that like Him someday I will be.13*

Big Sister

"God sets the solitary in families; He brings out those who are bound, into prosperity" (Psalm 68:6a).

Many of the changes that were taking place in Iris' life go back to the times she spent in the Beasley home. She took advantage of every opportunity she had to be a part of their lives, sometimes staying for a day or two or for up to two weeks. It was during these visits that she was not only ministered to spiritually by Bro. Manley and Marthé, but it was a time when she discovered that being a Christian doesn't mean that you can't have fun. And fun she had, especially with Jonathan who had just turned thirteen when his parents announced:

'Son, we've invited a lady who has lived a pretty rough life, and who has been in prison, to hang out with us for a little while. We want you to help us minister to her. Her name is Iris.'

Jonathan remembers
"In walks Iris. She was taller than my Dad and when she saw me, she engulfed me with a big ole hug and acted like I was her long-lost brother. It didn't take long for us to really hit it off because the childhood she hadn't experienced, due to her choosing the lifestyle she did at the age of thirteen, she began reliving with me. She had a lot of catching up to do.

"We played tricks on each other, which Mother and Dad also enjoyed participating in. I'll never forget the morning when Iris was lying there, sound asleep, with her mouth wide open, that my Dad got a water pistol and squirted water down her throat. I know this probably will shock some folk who have been so profoundly touched by my father's life and message, but don't forget that he didn't get to live a "normal" childhood either, because of the choices he had made as a teenager.

"This was just a part of life with the Beasleys. Between those serious times when Iris sat (literally) at my father's feet, listening to him talk about what it meant to walk by faith, she and I would be horse-playing around. One time we got to chasing each other around the house and ended up running through the guest bedroom, smashing into the bed, which broke into pieces. Mother tried to be upset, but instead of tears we all ended up laughing.

"Those things were fun, but what I recall the most was watching Iris grow in Christ through those years, as well as the counsel she had for me out of the lessons she had learned the hard way. Whenever she observed even a hint of my having an attitude toward my parents she would speak to me privately. She would tell me how her problems had started with an attitude toward her parents, and against authority in general. She'd point out how my Mom and Dad were doing all they could to provide a healthy home environment for us kids, and even though they might not always understand what I was going through, they loved me and wanted God's best for me.

"It was like having another sibling in the family, as I was the only child still living at home for most of those years. Iris came in and out of my life on a regular basis, checking on me, counseling when needed, and generally acting as another big sister. We watched her faith grow along the lines of my Dad. We saw her ministry begin to be established as she started traveling and sharing her testimony. Sometimes she'd go with my mother on one of her speaking engagements and sometimes mother would accompany Iris on one of her invitations, all the time trying to teach Iris "how to be a lady." At times these experiences were quite amusing as Iris had an old vocabulary to forget, and an entirely new one to learn. She would sometimes unintentionally embarrass my mother, such as the time mother had gone with her to this church where she was going to give her testimony.

On the way, mother had reminded Iris to use the term, "house of ill repute," rather than "whore house," as she was prone to say. Iris actually did not understand why saying that term was wrong since my father had told her that it was a perfectly good word found in the King James Bible, which was the version Iris used. In any case, Iris stopped in the middle of her testimony, looked at mother who was sitting in the second row, and said: *"Marthé, what was it you told me to say instead of "whore house?"* They had a good laugh later, but at that moment mother could have crawled under the pew.

"During the summer of 1983, when I was attending Baylor University and playing football, my Dad arranged for me to spend 6 weeks ministering with Iris in Europe. We spoke in US military base junior and high school assemblies all over Germany during the day, and in churches at night. I shared from the perspective of a pretty straight living athlete who grew up in a Christian home, and Iris shared from her totally opposite kind of lifestyle that involved all the perverted things she had gotten into. We presented a clear choice of life, the contrast between good and evil, a God-centered life and a life of drugs, prostitution and crime.

Interestingly, the questions we were asked afterward from the students were addressed as much to me as Iris. Kids wanted to know how I managed to stay pure and not get involved in what so many of them were already into as teenagers.

"I'll never forget those six weeks of fun and ministry together. Iris admired the path I had chosen to take, and delighted in telling the kids that she had been around someone who did make the right choices. We both emphasized that it was the same grace and love that accompanied me on the road I had taken, as the grace and love that had followed her and protected her during those years when she could have destroyed herself. And it was that same grace and love that eventually transformed her life.

"When Blue came into Iris' life it was like watching one of my own sisters process what was happening. We had talked about what we were looking for in a mate, and now, here Iris was faced with actual choices to make. Initially, when Blue arrived, he was a diamond in the rough, but little by little we watched God change him into the vessel of honor we now know him to be.

"To watch two people whose lives had been lived as far from God as you can go, come together by God's grace, pure before Him and before each other, has been one of the most fulfilling experiences of my life. And now, having watched them over the years, I can honestly say that, I have never known a woman of faith like Iris, and Blue is right there with her. The only other person I know who has set such a high standard of the faith is the one who taught them the faith walk from the beginning, and I am proud to call him, "Dad."

Deborah (Debbie) remembers

"My parents had been telling me about Iris and I was looking forward to meeting her when I returned home from Alaska where I had spent the summer with my brother, Manley Jr. who was pastoring in the Anchorage area. It was not long before my heart bonded with my "new sister" and I soon found myself traveling with her from time to time on ministry engagements. She was still adjusting to the difference there was between her new way of life and the lost years of her past. She had never experienced what we would call a normal youth, since from her young teenage years she had lived as abnormal a life as a child could live. And then, of course, there were all those years in prison when the outside world was passing her by.

"My role in her life became, and pretty much still is, to be a listening ear and a counselor. We've shared many precious hours talking and praying together. And of course, we've also had fun, especially if my mother is anywhere around! Then also, I think I've kind of filled the void that was left when my Dad passed away. Iris will call, we'll talk...I'm usually the Beasley who will say, *'Now Iris, you need to...don't allow that to...be careful...'* and so on.

"Then there's been the impact she has made on my life and the lessons I've learned as I've watched someone live a life of total reliance on God, the kind of living that is not that often seen these days. I don't think I know anyone who holds on so lightly to what they have. We laugh about it but, it sometimes seems as though she and Blue give more away than they receive, yet they end up being taken care of.

My niece Candace, who was in nursing school some years back, was on her way to visit me when she totaled her car. To her surprise, her insurance had run out three days before and she had no money to buy another vehicle. We were all trying to figure out what we could do when we got a phone call from Iris.

What's going on, Debbie?"
"What do you mean, what's going on?"
"Well something must be going on because the Lord has laid it on our hearts to give you our car."
"Let me let you talk to Candace."

"Candace ended up with a car that took her all the way through school and beyond, and, should we be surprised, Iris and Blue were given an even better car than they had given to Candace. This had a profound impact on my niece who saw first hand, a dimension of faith that you don't see every day.

"Over the years that I've known Iris there has been a growing awareness that the same grace that changed Iris is the grace that has held on to me. This was driven home one time when we were together in the Denton, Texas area, where a number of churches had scheduled a joint Sunday evening service where Iris would give her testimony. To promote the event, they asked Iris to visit each of churches during the Sunday morning worship hour to give a brief word that would encourage the people to attend the evening meeting. I was with her, and this meant that we had to race from one church to the next, all in an hour's time. There were at least six churches to cover. I'll never forget one of those stops.

"We arrived right in the middle of some very upbeat worship and no one noticed us as we made our way to the front row. The pastor finally saw us and excitedly announced to the congregation: "*Iris Urrey is here. She's the one who was a prostitute, had many abortions, was hooked on drugs and ended up spending years in prison. She's here to say a word, and tonight she will be telling her whole story. You won't want to miss it.*" Then, looking straight at me, he said: "*Iris, come up here and share with us.*"

"I was shaken. He thought I was the former drug addict and ex-con. Iris of course got up, smiling from ear to ear, and went to the podium while I sat there processing what had just happened. But the more I thought about it the more I realized I had just been taught two things.

"**First:** The work God does in a person's life is the same, no matter how good or bad we have been in the past. Anyone looking at us could not tell the difference—could not tell who had lived the life the pastor had described, and who had not.

"**Second:** But for God's grace I could have been the ex-con who had been a prostitute, who had aborted all those babies, who had been on drugs and who had spent eight years in prison. That could have been me. That could have been me…"

And that could have been any of us.

Lady Iris Heads West

He leadeth me, O blessed thought!
O words with heavenly comfort fraught.
Whate'er I do, where'er I be, Still 'tis God's hand that leadeth me. 14

Iris' world was spinning after things fell apart between the church and Crossway Manor. She rented a trailer near Hobby Airport, not far from where her sister, Punkin, lived, and Virgil Weekly, the owner of the Cimarron Paving Company, who had been paying the utility bills at Crossway, provided her with furniture. She didn't know what was going to happen next, but the daily phone conversations with Bro. Manley and the encouragement from Mickey Bonner, helped keep her going.

She hadn't lived in that apartment but a few weeks, however, when a letter arrived from a lady in Chandler, Arizona, inviting Iris to join her in a prison ministry God had raised up in the Phoenix area. Sensing that this was of the Lord, and with the encouragement of Manley Beasley, she headed west, with all her worldly goods loaded in the back of a small rental truck. It was a step of faith to leave the familiar surroundings of the Houston area with little cash and, due to her ex-con status, no credit card. But the walk of faith she was learning from Bro. Manley was the life she had committed herself to live.

As she drove west she had time to think back on all that God had done for her in the relatively brief time since she had met him on that Telephone Road sidewalk. Now, heading into the sunset, she began anticipating what God might have in store for her in a place she knew nothing about. As is always the case, however, with God's children who are on pilgrimage with Him, He had gone ahead to prepare the way. Within the first 24 hours Iris had been offered a three bedroom house with den, large living room and pool, rent free for 6 months. The man who had pre-paid 6 months rent on this house discovered too late that his wife was allergic to something in the building and they had to vacate immediately when she had a very serious allergy attack. And within that same 24 hour period another couple had given her a Volkswagen Beetle to drive, just another confirmation that God was watching over His child.

God's provision, however, was soon to reach beyond housing, transportation and prison ministry. He knew she was still hurting from the experience of losing *Crossway Manor* and that she needed family, so, God brought into her life Harold and Linn Green, who had given her the Volkswagen. Harold had been a longtime friend of Bro. Manley's, so knowing Harold was on the staff of *North Phoenix Baptist Church,* Manley had phoned to tell him about Iris and to let him know that he had asked Iris to call him. She did, and it was not long before she was spending as much time at their place as her own. They loved her, affirmed her and treated her as a daughter, and little by little, through them and others of the North Phoenix Church congregation the restoring and renewing she needed began taking place.

Another affirmation that God had not forgotten her were the invitations she began to again receive, invitations to share her testimony, not only in the Phoenix area, but beyond. This was another spirit-booster in light of her ministry calendar having been wiped clean after she had been asked to close the girl's home. One of these ministry opportunities involved a community-wide evangelistic outreach effort sponsored by several Phoenix churches, including *North Phoenix Baptist* where Iris worshiped. It was to be an all day event where big name sporting and entertainment personalities would be singing and giving their testimonies. They asked Iris to share her testimony, to which she agreed, that is, until she heard that she would be on stage with a recent Miss America. Iris picks up the story.

"An issue I have struggled with all my life is something that I find many others face. I'm talking about not liking yourself—not liking 'me.' I'm talking about being able to accept yourself for who you are. I don't mean the 'I'm OK, you're OK' junk, but seeing yourself as someone God made and that He didn't make a mistake. **You're not a freak. You're not an accident. God designed you and He has a purpose for your life.**

"This is one of the biggest hurdles and the biggest acts of faith I have had to deal with, and sometimes still do. There has never been a 'one time' experience when God has set me free from it. It is something He allows me to deal with to this day. Anyway, when I heard about my being on stage with Miss America, I backed out. I told them I didn't want to do that. There it was again. The old, *'I don't like me'* thing. *'Oh,'* they said. *'Miss America is going to give her testimony in the morning part of the program. We'll break for lunch, then in the afternoon you will speak right before Richard Jackson brings the closing message.'*

"I still wasn't sure, but felt less uptight with this arrangement, that is, until we arrived at the auditorium. I was told that they had just heard that Miss America's flight had been delayed and she was not going to be able to make it in time for her scheduled spot on the program, and they wanted me to take her place. The first thing I thought was, *'Everyone has read their program and they are looking forward to hearing Miss America. What were they going to think when I walk out. Who's she?'* I began to struggle with who I was.

"But as I stepped onto the stage, God took over. I became satisfied with who I was in God's sight and left the rest to Him. I shared my story, then I decided to tell them what I had just been going through, and how from my childhood I had had trouble with accepting who I was, of liking me just like God had made me. I told them I had been fighting this when I was asked to take the place of someone as beautiful as Miss America. What I didn't know was that Miss America had actually arrived in time to hear me talk about the issue of not being able to accept ourselves, of liking ourselves as God has made us. She had been listening.

"When I finished and went backstage, to my surprise, there stood Miss America, and before I could say anything she came over, hugged me and began to weep.

'I've had a complex all my life,' she said. *'I've never felt that anybody liked me for me, for who I am, as a person, not for just how I look. Because of this I've had trouble accepting myself.'* That day the Lord showed me that, even though it sometimes does not make sense, there are a lot of people who are hurting, who are struggling with just liking themselves.

"When I talk about this in meetings, so many women come up to tell me how they secretly struggle with the same thing. As you are reading this book you may be saying, *'That's where I am, Iris.'* Well, listen...

"When I look in the mirror some mornings I have to remind myself of Psalm 45: 10 where it talks about *'the king desiring my beauty.'* I have to go on what the Bible says about me and not on how I feel. One of the biggest hurdles I face is getting people to really believe what God's Word says about them and not what they think about themselves.

"In Psalm 139: 14 it says that I am fearfully and wonderfully made. Matthew 10:30 says that even the hairs on my head are numbered. It says in Psalm 139:3 that God is acquainted with all my ways. In Romans 8:31 the Apostle Paul asks, *"If God be for us, who can be against us?*" and that includes your feelings. Ephesians 2:10 reminds us that we are God's workmanship, and in Colossians 1:22 that we are going to be presented holy and without blemish to God.

"Men and women struggle with believing how special they are; how unique they are in God's sight. And that is what really matters. We were so special that Jesus, who never cussed like I did, who never got strung out on heroin like I did, who never robbed or did any of the filthy things that I did, was willing to become sin for me. When He was praying in the garden of Gethsemane and was told by His Father that the only way He could finish the work He had been sent to do was to carry all my sins in His body on the cross, I can almost hear Him say to His Father: *'If there is no other way for me to save Iris Urrey, I am willing to become sin for her.'* The pure, sinless Son of God became sin for me. That's how special I am. That's how special you are!

"If you go on your feelings they will mess you up. You have to decide on a daily basis to believe what God says about you. Don't let the person looking at you in the mirror defeat you. Tell that person how special and unique you are to the One who created you. Remind that person what Jesus did for you, because if you doubt that you are special to God it is going to affect every area of your life. It will affect your witnessing and it will affect your ability to really trust Him. If you don't want to end up being programmed by the world, remind that person in the mirror what God says about you.

> *Oh Lord, you have examined my heart and know everything*
> *about me. You know when I sit down or when I stand up. You*
> *know my every thought when far away. You chart the path*
> *ahead of me and tell me where to stop and rest.*
> *Every moment*
> *You know where I am. You know what I am going to say, even*
> *before I say it, Lord. You both precede me and follow me. You*
> *place your hand of blessing on my head. Such knowledge is too*
> *wonderful for me, too great for me to know!*
> *I can never escape*

*from your spirit! I can never get away from your presence! If I
go up to heaven, You are there. If I go down to the place of the
dead, You are there. If I ride the wings of the morning, if I dwell
by the farthest oceans, even there your hand will guide me, and
your strength will support me (Psalm 139:1-10, NLT).*

What is Victory?

"Victory is having said of you what is written of you." —*Manley Beasley*

In the spring of 1980, Bro. Manley and Glenn Sheppard flew to Phoenix, Arizona, to participate in Iris' *Mission Service Corps Volunteer* commissioning service held at North Phoenix Baptist Church. She was the 479th[15] volunteer and at that moment could not have anticipated one day becoming the longest serving MSCV in Southern Baptist history, a relationship that continues to this day.

Manley and Glenn felt that now that Iris had this relationship with what was then the Home Mission Board of the SBC, that she needed to move back east, so it was not long before she was heading for Atlanta. On her way, she stopped over in Dallas where her friend Carlos McLeod, director of the Texas Baptist Evangelism Department, had invited her to give her testimony at their annual Conference. Iris recalls...

"It was being held in this huge arena with such a big crowd that it would have been impossible to find a family member, or your best friend, if you tried. I was sitting near the front, waiting to give my testimony when, for some reason, I turned around and looked straight into the eyes of the pastor of the church that had let me go. In that crowd of thousands of people there he was, right behind me. I got so excited. I jumped up, went to him, gave him a big hug and told him I loved him. I asked how his wife and kids were, then all of a sudden I realized that I wasn't mad any more. I felt no bitterness—it was all gone!"

After that session Iris ran straight to her room in the hotel across the street from the Convention Center. She had given Manley Beasley, and his wife Marthé, the key to her room as he was not feeling well, and being able to rest that close to the conference was a lot better than his having to drive thirty minutes to where they lived in Euless. She knocked on the door. Marthé answered.

Iris rushed into the room shouting, *"Bro. Manley, Bro. Manley, I'm free. I'm free. I have the victory!"* Manley, knowing exactly what she was referring to, looked out from under the covers and said: *"Well, I'm glad you have the victory, but I haven't respected that preacher since it happened."*

"Well, good night!" Iris said.
'Now Iris,' he replied. *"Not respecting someone is different than being bitter.'*
They had a good laugh.

"From the time I had left that church, to the time I saw that pastor at the Evangelism Conference, a full year and a half had passed," recalls Iris. "It took that long for me to get victory over my bitterness. I'm so thankful that Bro. Manley never gave up on me. He kept calling; *'Iris, do have the victory yet?'* It helped me understand what he was meaning when he preached on *What is Victory?* at North Phoenix Baptist the Sunday I was commissioned. He asked the question, *'What is victory?'* I came up with all kinds of answers, not even coming close to his definition. Then he said: **'Victory is having said of you what is written of you.'** He described what Scripture says about God's children, who they are, what they look like, and how they act. He asked the congregation if it was being said of North Phoenix Baptist what was written of it in the Bible.

"Bro. Manley showed us where it says we are **more than conquerors** through Christ who loved us...' (Romans 8:37). Victory is living that kind of life.

"He read where the Bible says we are **saints,** which means we are a holy people.' Victory is people noticing that we are different, that we don't think, talk or act like the world does. *'Is that what is being said of you and this church?'* he asked.

"Bro. Manley showed us where we are called **priests,** that we are part of a royal priesthood (1Peter 2:9). He explained that a priest is a 'go-between,' someone who reaches up to God and all His supply with one hand and with the other hand reaches out to someone in need and brings the two together. Victory is performing our duties as priests. He asked, '*Are the members of North Phoenix performing the duties of a priest? Is that what people think about you and your church?*' I thought, '*Is that what people think about me?*'

"This is something we all have to keep learning. It's a continuous process. I still am learning, sometimes the hard way," Iris confesses. "But I'm so thankful that God doesn't give up on me—that He keeps changing me, little by little. I'm not there yet, but one day like Him I will be!"

This has been the passion of Iris' life, to have said of her what is written of her in the Bible—to become more and more like the person Scripture describes. This, and the transparency of her life, the simplicity of her faith and her sensitivity to the needs of others, has led to people feeling that they can share with her their innermost fears and struggles. This we find in the following testimony by Paula Edney.

A Testimony

Paula Edney

*Assistant professor of Health and Wellness, Gainsville State
College, Georgia; 19 years college basketball coach, 5 years
Head Coach with Athletes in Action and Head Coach for the
1985 USA Pan Am Games' Ladies Basketball team.*

"I'll never forget 1981. On April 4th of that year my Mom died suddenly. She and I were very close so her death "rocked my world" in indescribable ways. But something else happened that summer that changed my life in a way that continues to affect all that I do to this day. It happened at a *Fellowship of Christian Athletes* camp in Black Mountain, NC, when I heard Iris' story.

"I had been asked by a Christian friend to be the basketball counselor at the camp that summer. I thought I was a Christian and I had always talked to my players about God and Christ, so I thought this was a good idea. Even though my life was full of sin, I gave no thought to that fact because I expected that I would find a whole lot of other people at the camp just like me.

"I remember it well. I was sitting in the main auditorium with approximately 300 junior high and high school girls waiting for the introduction of our guest speaker for the day. A few moments later Iris Urrey walked to the stage and began telling her story. Immediately I could see something different in Iris but I didn't think much about it, though I was absolutely captivated by what she was saying, as was everyone else in the building. The impact it was having, however, only became obvious when Iris gave an invitation for us to give our lives to Jesus. As she started singing, almost everyone was crying and when she asked those who had made the decision to turn their lives over to Christ, to step forward, an incredible thing happened. Girls began to pour down the aisles! What I didn't realize until later was that I was the only counselor to go forward. It was at this point that my life began to take a dramatic turn.

"I was so touched by Iris' story, her personality and commitment to Christ, I knew I had to get to know her better. Little did I realize that God already had that planned. I was asked to take Iris to the airport the next morning. We had a great time. She said she'd be glad to stay in touch, which delighted me. I knew, however, how much she travelled so I didn't expect to have much contact. To my surprise, I received a postcard from her a few months later, inviting me to come for a visit during the Christmas holidays. I was so excited to have the opportunity to see her again.

"When I arrived we didn't do anything special; we just spent a lot of time talking and getting to know each other. Iris' life and story was continuing to impact me. Iris was a good listener and as I began to share I felt that I could tell her anything, and before I knew it, I began telling her about what I now call, "my lifestyle of sin." What was interesting is that Iris didn't act shocked or even surprised—we just continued talking. Later that day we ran some errands and went out for a pizza, and when we returned to her house we began talking about the Bible and what it said about sin, what it meant to be a Christian, and so many things that I had not understood about living your life for Jesus.

"That night I went to bed knowing my life had to change, but I was going through such a mighty struggle. For 13 years I had lived this lifestyle, making all my own decisions while thinking I had given my life to Christ. Up until then, as far as I was concerned, everything was OK between Jesus and me. But when I thought about what Iris and I had talked about I was really shaken and confused. I got my Bible out and began to read, hoping I could make sense of it all and that's exactly what happened.

"Every verse I turned to spoke to some aspect of my life and how it needed correcting. I began to clearly see, for the first time, that God's will for my life was not what I had been deceived into believing it was. My heart was breaking. I had been wrong all this time. I had hurt and negatively influenced so many others. I cried myself to sleep that night.

"When I awoke the next morning I could hear Iris in the kitchen. I still felt like crying and didn't know how I was going to be able to talk to her, but I got dressed and went out to the kitchen anyway. Iris said: *"Good morning."* It was all I could do to get anything out and Iris knew immediately that something was going on. The only thing I remember her saying was, *"Paula, are you ready to give your life to Christ?"* At that point I lost it. I started sobbing and Iris knew the Holy Spirit had been working on me all night (and obviously before that as well) so she let me calm down and then led me in a prayer. At that moment I REALLY gave my life to Jesus Christ.

"I can't begin to tell you all the ways Christ has blessed my life—sometimes I think I could write a book about it all. One thing I can tell you is that I owe a tremendous debt of gratitude to Iris. I could never thank her enough for allowing Jesus to manifest Himself in her in such a way that I could really see Him. When I first heard her I knew that Jesus was alive and well, but now, I can testify that He's alive and well in my life as well, even to this day, 28 years later!

Trapped in Denial

*Denial: A defense mechanism in which confrontation with
reality is avoided by denying the existence of a problem.*
—*Webster's dictionary*

For eight years the Urrey home had been anything but a joyful place to live.
Iris was in prison and her mother, Mirrell, was living in denial, forbidding
family members to say anything about Iris' imprisonment, while telling
everyone that her daughter was working in the Coca Cola Bottling Plant in
San Antonio.

A cloud had settled over the Urrey household and Mirrell was becoming more
and more of a recluse. She stopped attending the Ladies Sunday School class
where she had friends who went back, almost to her childhood. She would
only attend the Sunday morning worship service, sit at the back, and leave
during the invitation because she didn't want to talk to anyone. A cloud of
denial followed her everywhere she went. She avoided conversations that had
anything to do with family, especially about Iris, her third child.

When Iris was released from prison, her mother had told her what she was to
say. *"Tell them that you have been working in San Antonio and never tell anyone
that you have been in prison."* This made Iris very angry. She realized that her
mother was more concerned about her own reputation than in telling the
truth. Months later, when Iris had returned to the house for something, her
mother, again, reminded her that no one knew where she had been and that
Iris was not to ever mention prison to anyone.

This was more than Iris could handle. She cussed her mother out, then went through the house tearing up every picture that had ever been made of her. (Few pictures have been found to this day of Iris' early years) She then stuck her finger in her mother's face and said: *"Why would I ever want what you've got? You've never smoked a cigarette or done any of the things that I've done, and you're miserable. If God can't help you, what could He ever do for me? You need to smoke some marijuana before you go to church next Sunday morning and it might make you happy. The preacher would appreciate a smile instead of the sad face he sees every week."* With that, Iris stormed out of the house and headed back to Telephone Road.

A transforming mercy

Mirrell Urrey began to sob as she watched her daughter leave. She ran to her bedroom, fell on her knees and began to cry out to God. She recalls weeping for hours. She had come to the end of herself. She remembers telling God that her daughter had been in prison, as if God didn't know. Mirrell actually thought that she had been able to keep the truth away from Him. She told God how wrong she had been. She asked His forgiveness. In her mind's eye she placed Iris in one of her hands and her youngest daughter, Punkin, in the other, as she raised them toward heaven.

"Here are my daughters, God. I give them to you for whatever you want to do with them." When she rose from her knees that afternoon, the huge weight of dishonesty and denial that had been hanging around her neck for so long was gone. She was free.

The next Sunday, to the surprise of her Sunday School friends, in walked Mirrell. She had not been there in years. *"Mirrell, we're so glad to see you. We've missed you. How's the family?"* Mirrell took a deep breath:

"I've come to tell you that I'm a phony. I told you that Iris has been working at the Coca Cola Bottling Plant in San Antonio. I lied. My daughter has been in prison for eight years. She's a heroin addict and she's been living in sin ever since she was released over a year ago. I don't know all that she's been into and I don't want to know, but I want to ask your forgiveness for not telling you the truth and I want to say that if Iris never changes, it is going to be my fault."

"Well, Mirrell, we knew all along that Iris was in prison. It was in all the papers. We just didn't want to say anything to you about it because we knew you were trying to keep it a secret. We didn't want to embarrass you."

Mirrell Urrey looked at her friends in disbelief. *"Ya'll knew? You knew all along and didn't say anything to me?"* *"Well, you know how it is, Mirrell. We thought that it was better to just leave you alone. We didn't want to upset you or embarrass you. You know how it is sometimes…it's difficult…well, you know."*

It was difficult for Mirrell Urrey to understand how her friends knew what she had been facing for all those years, yet none of them had reached out to help her. But that's how it is sometimes, or even often is in the church family—**a code of silence.**

The code of silence may be due to fear. Sometimes it's due to not wanting to get involved in someone else's life, or simply not being willing to take the time. It may be out of a sense that they themselves wouldn't know what to say or do. It sometimes is because they are harboring their own secrets.

But Mirrell was past that now. She had gone to church that morning with the resolve to come clean by telling the whole church that she had been living a lie. When the worship service time arrived she walked right past the back pew, where she had been sitting for years, and headed straight for the second row from the front. Everything was now different. It seemed to her that the pastor was preaching an unusually fine message that morning. The truth was, she was listening with a new set of ears. She had been freed from the bondage of denial. When the invitation to respond was extended at the end of the sermon, Mirrell Urrey was the first one to walk forward to take the pastor's hand.

"I've been living a lie for over eight years," she told him. *"I've been telling everyone that Iris was working in San Antonio when she was really in prison. I'm so sorry."*

To Mirrell's surprise, the pastor said: *"Mirrell, I've known that all along and I should have reached out to you, but I thought you would be embarrassed. Please forgive me. Here, take this microphone and while I ask God to forgive me, you tell the congregation what you have told me."*

Mirrell looked into the faces of the church family she had been a part of for so many years, and through tears said: *"I've been living a lie. I've been telling you that my daughter Iris has been working in a Coca Cola bottling plant in San Antonio when she really was in prison for eight years, and since they let her out she's been living in all kinds of sin. She's a heroin addict and I don't know what to do."*

Mirrell had no sooner spoken those words than a woman near the back called out. *"I've been lying too. I've been telling you that my son is in the Marines, but he's not. He's in prison. I've been too embarrassed to let anybody know. I'm so sorry. Please pray for my son."*

In addition to the tears being shed by almost everyone in attendance that morning, and along with the hugs and promises to pray and help in whatever way they could, two miracles were being set in motion that can only be explained as the activity of God, in response to two mothers getting their hearts right with Him.

Seven days later, retired NFL Cleveland Browns football great, Bill Glass, began his prison ministry, holding a crusade in *The Walls,* in Huntsville, Texas. As Bill invited the inmates to turn their lives over to Jesus Christ, a young man, whom many back home thought was serving in the Marines, stepped forward.

Eleven days later, on a sidewalk in front of a topless bar, an "incorrigible" young woman, an ex-con, drug addict and prostitute, ***knelt down a tramp and stood up a lady.***

Free at Last

"You shall know the truth and the truth shall make you free" (John 8:32).

Things were different now in the Urrey household. Iris' mother was no longer living under a cloud of denial. She was free! And with this freedom came the desire to help others who were in a similar situation she had lived with for years. She knew there were many parents who were struggling with the embarrassment and hurt of having a wayward child, while some were resorting to the false security of denial as she had done. Mirrell determined that, though no one had reached out to her, she was going to make it a point to help as many of these parents and children as she could.

She became convicted that missions was not just something you only gave money to, but it was something you *did*, so Mirrell Urrey set out on mission. She told Iris and her siblings, her grandchildren, and her husband, to find as many of these wayward children as they could and to *bring them to her.* It was not long before the Urrey home would be turned into a lighthouse and refuge.

"Mama couldn't wait for holiday times when the house would be full of family and guests," Iris recalls. "She even looked forward to the visits of Mormons and Jehovah Witnesses. She'd overwhelm them with kindness, welcoming them with a hug and sometimes inviting them to stay for a meal, or at least to have a refreshment, all the time showing and sharing her love for Jesus."

Mirrell on radio

Iris was in Chicago, IL, being interviewed on a two hour call-in program on the Moody Broadcasting Network. After giving her testimony the calls began to pour in, and interestingly, many of them had to do with her mother and how she had coped with all that Iris had put her through. The program host finally said to Iris: *"Let's see if we can get your mother on the phone and let her respond directly to some of these callers,"* so they phoned Mirrell Urrey in Outlaw Bend, near Hoop N Holler, Texas.

"Mama, this is Iris. I'm on a call-in radio program up here in Chicago. The people here want to hook you up by phone with the callers who are asking how you managed to make it, having a daughter like me. We'll call you back in a couple minutes, so Mama, go quick and put on your lipstick because when we call back you'll be live on radio." Iris, of course, was teasing, but without thinking, Mirrell put on her lipstick and did her best to quickly fix herself up before she went on "live radio!"

R-i-n-g... R-i-n-g
"Hello."
"Mrs. Urrey, we have callers waiting who would like to ask you some questions about how you managed when Iris was running away from God."

Mirrell started out real quiet like, but soon she became animated. *"Now you listen, I want to tell you...you don't give up on your child, you love 'em. It's easy for some folk to talk about "tough love," but you listen. That's your baby and you'd better love 'em even when they are being their worst."*

The announcer interrupted to say that they were needing to take a one minute break before continuing with the questions, but Mirrell, who was right in the middle of something she thought was very important said, *'You listen young man. You just hold off until I'm finished.'* Mirrell took the program over, which was not at all like her personality. That day she became an ambassador for "not giving up on your children when the situation looks its darkest."

According to the station manager, that particular program with Iris had more callers than any of their previous ones, which had included many of America's best known Christian personalities.

A Miracle of Grace

Amazing grace, how sweet the sound
that saved a wretch like me—John Newton

The ministry to wayward girls at Crossway Manor had been occupying much of Iris' time, but when she was forced to shut the work down, she entered a very difficult period of feeling rejected by the Christian community. She wondered if the Lord would ever be able to use her again. She struggled with self-worth and was still wrestling with these negative thoughts the morning she stood in front of the mirror in the trailer she had moved to near Hobby Airport. As she stood looking at herself she began talking:

"They may have made me close my ministry at Crossway Manor and nobody may love me, but I know someone who does. Jesus does. I was lost and He saved me. I was a drug addict and a prostitute and He delivered me. I was in prison and He freed me."

As she reminded herself of the miraculous change that had taken place in her life she began sensing a strong urge to go outside and tell everyone she could find what God had done. She started knocking on doors. She went from one house to the next. She recalls that sharing her testimony in this way was as much for her benefit as it was for those who listened to her.

"It made me feel happy. I was reminding myself of what God had done in my life. *'Hello. I'm your neighbor from down the street. I'd like to tell you what Jesus has done for me.'*"

Iris doesn't know what impact her testimony had on anyone else that day, but she'll never forget what did happen when she knocked on one of the doors. *"Oh, please come in,"* the lady said. *"Please come in, I've been waiting for you."* Iris sensed that something unusual was happening. As she sat down, the lady got her Bible and turned to 1 Corinthians 6 and showed Iris what she had written beside verse 9; *"Homosexuality is sin."* She then turned to the passage in 1 Thessalonians 5:23 where it talks about our being preserved, or presented, blameless at the coming of the Lord Jesus. Beside that Scripture she had written, *"Sammy is going to be saved before I die and will be presented blameless to the Lord when he dies."*

This mother, who had been waiting for the Lord to send her someone she could talk with, looked at Iris and said; *"Will you witness to my son when he comes to visit me?"* *"Sure,"* Iris said. *"When did you last see him?"* *"Oh,"* she said. *"It must be five or six years."* *"Six years? That's a long time. Tell me about him."*

"His name is Sammy Barrett. He is one of the top male models in New York City." She then began leading Iris through her home, showing her posters and pictures of Sammy hanging on every wall. He was a strikingly handsome figure, dressed in his trademark white suit, holding various products. *"He is the male model for Smirnoff-Vodka and Red Breast Irish Whiskey"* she said, pointing to two posters. *"His picture is on magazine covers and billboards, but behind all of this, he is one of the main leaders of the gay-lesbian movement in New York City."*

Sammy's mother went on to tell Iris of the many surgeries she had been through and how she was praying that Sammy would soon visit her because she did not know how long she had to live. In the meantime, she was holding on to the promise she felt God had given her that Sammy would be saved before she died. They talked a while, then Iris prayed with her before returning to her trailer. *"That poor lady,"* she thought. *"She is so ill and her son doesn't even visit her."*

The next morning the phone rang. *"Iris. He's here. He's here! Sammy is here!* He had suddenly shown up, unannounced. It was his first visit in over five years. *"Can you come over?"*

"We hit it right off," Iris recalls. "God allowed us to connect in a way only He could do. It was like we were best friends. It was like we had known each other forever. Blue says I have a 'gay magnate.' I think it's because they know I receive them as they are and don't come across with condemning vibes. Anyway, since it was Christmas time I invited Sammy to join me and my family for Christmas eve at my parent's home in Outlaw Bend, Texas. Christmas eve was when we exchanged gifts and shared what God had been doing in our lives over the past year. Since this was a good distance from his mother's place, I suggested Sammy stay overnight before driving back to celebrate Christmas with her."

Now, this is where it got interesting. The Urrey house had three bedrooms and at Christmas time the place was full. Iris' mother would put all the girls in one room and all the boys in another; so Ernest, Iris' older brother, who was paranoid about being around gays, had to sleep in the same room with Sammy. He stayed awake all night. He didn't sleep a wink and the next morning he took Iris outside. He said:

"I can show you in the Bible where homosexuals can't go to heaven. Why did you bring him here?" Iris replied: *"Jug, (Ernest's nickname) if that's so, then I'll never be able to go to heaven. If they can't get saved, then I can't get saved. But that's not true because I can't find any sin in the Bible that Jesus' blood won't wash away."* That's the last time Ernest ever mentioned it.

"We had a great time," Iris remembers. "Sammy heard the testimonies of how God had changed our lives and how special Christmas was to us, then, after spending a couple days celebrating with his mother, he returned to New York City to pick up his career. He didn't respond to our witness at that time, and I didn't know if I would ever see him again, but I could tell something was happening. I kept praying."

A year later
It was not long after this that Iris moved to Phoenix. She did not return to Texas until the following Christmas. She phoned Mrs. Barrett to see how she was doing and to her surprise was told that Sammy had just flown down from New York to visit his mother again. It didn't take Iris long to drive down to Mrs. Barrett's house where she and Sammy picked up where they had left off.

Though his mother's physical condition was a good deal worse than when he had seen her the year before, you would never have guessed it from the way Sammy was acting. In an attempt to brighten his mother up he began gently waltzing her around the room as he sang, *"I want to stroll all over heaven with you."* Suddenly his mother gasped and fell to the floor. They rushed her to the hospital where she was immediately put in Intensive Care. Iris and Sammy anxiously waited.

They had not been there long before the doctor came out to share the bad news: *'Mr. Barrett, we're so sorry. Your mother did not make it.'* As he turned to leave, the ICU nurse ran in. *"Doctor, Mrs. Barrett's heart is beating again."* To everyone's surprise, this happened a second and a third time. Neither the doctor nor the nurse could explain why her vital signs kept returning. Iris, however, thought she might know.

"Sammy, your mother told me that God promised her that you would be saved before she died. I saw where she had written those very words in her Bible. Sammy, I think maybe that's why this is happening. She's waiting for you..." With that, Sammy, already under conviction, fell to his knees right there in the waiting room in front of everyone. When he stood up a few minutes later, he stood up a new creation. The doctor returned to ask Sammy and Iris to join him in the Intensive Care Unit. As the doctor, nurse and Iris watched, Sammy took his mother's hand, leaned over and whispered in her ear, *"Mama, you can let go now because I've met Jesus and one day I'll be following you to heaven."*

Iris will never forget what happened next. With all the tubes and paraphernalia attached to her body, and not having been able to communicate since she had arrived at the hospital, Sammy's mother found the strength to raise her hands upward, as though in an act of thanksgiving to her Lord. Then, as her hands dropped back to her side, her spirit soared heavenward.

The genuineness of his conversion was soon evident when Sammy returned to New York City. He gave up his modeling career and never went back to his gay friends, other than to share with them what had happened to him. He began preaching on the street in front of Rockefeller Center and it would not be long before Sammy would have his own "street church," with a congregation of regulars who were made up of prostitutes, drug addicts, gays and lesbians. On one occasion, Iris joined him in his street ministry.

Word soon spread about Sammy's conversion and how God was using him for His glory in New York City. He began receiving letters and phone calls from concerned parents all across the country, asking him to try to reach their sons and daughters who had gone to New York to seek careers in modeling or acting. During that period it is estimated that Sammy personally sat at the bedside of over 100 young men and women as they died from Aids, other sexual diseases, or from drug overdoses.

Sammy would eventually marry, father two children, live a fulfilled life for a few years, then eventually succumb to the HIV virus, a result of his pre-conversion lifestyle. But only God knows how many, through his witness, will one day join him and his mother in heaven's celestial dance. And only God knows the part a faithful mother played in her son's being "presented blameless" before the Lord, by trusting God to fulfill the promise He had given her.

Iris Goes to Europe

Wherever He leads I'll go, I'll follow my Christ who loves me so,
Wherever He leads I'll go.16

The beautiful Swiss ski resort of Thyon 2000 with its magnificent views of the world-famous Matterhorn and Mont Blanc, Europe's highest peak, was the location of the 1979 *International Congress on Revival*. Being able to afford the trip was one of Iris's first major tests of faith in which she saw God miraculously provide the money. This was also the first time she would experience travelling internationally as an ex-con.

As exciting as it was to find herself in the beautiful land of snow, watches, cheese and chocolate, the greater joy was the fellowship with fellow believers from both the United States and Europe. Contacts were made that week that would ultimately lead to Europe becoming her home away from home for a three year period. It was here, high in the Alps, that Bob Ferguson—then pastor of Faith Baptist Church in Kaiserslautern, Germany—would hear Iris share her testimony and where he would first begin to consider inviting her to minister in the churches of the European Baptist Convention, of which he was president.

It was at the next ICR, in 1980, held in Interlaken, that Bob would ask Iris to pray about ministering in Europe. Having already met a number of the EBC pastors, and being told how effective her ministry could be, she agreed to pray. It soon became clear that this was a move she was to make; so Bob contacted the *Foreign Mission Board* of the Southern Baptist Convention to see if something might be arranged for her to work under its umbrella.

Due to extenuating matters, however—such as her being an ex-con and not having sufficient schooling in Baptist ways—they decided that it would not be appropriate for her to work with them.

Praying with Iris about discerning the Lord's will in this matter were Manley Beasley, Ron Dunn and Jack Taylor. These three men, seeing that the FMB would not sponsor her, recommended that a ministry board be formed to help guide her. They, along with layman Herb Peavey, became her board members. Now everything was in place for Iris to head for Europe. Realizing, however, that Iris had made an earlier commitment to serve as a Mission Service Corps Volunteer with the Home Mission Board, it was decided that she would divide her time into three month increments; three months in Europe, three months in America, for a three year period.

In a foreign land
Faith Baptist Church in Kaiserslautern, Germany, became Iris' European church family. They rented an apartment, purchased an automobile, and with the help of state-side friends whom God led to help support her, Iris' European ministry was launched. Pastor Bob Ferguson lined up the ministry engagements and generally watched out for her welfare. Yet, as exciting as ministering in EBC churches was, God would soon open a door for Iris that she would never have dreamed of—an open door that He had uniquely prepared her to walk through.

NATO
The *North Atlantic Treaty Organization* established in 1949 is a military alliance that consists of the United States and 18 other countries. It was originally formed to discourage Soviet Union aggression toward Western Europe. When Iris was ministering in Europe the Cold War was still in full swing and Ramstein, the largest and most strategic United Sates NATO Air Base, was located just 10 miles from Kaiserslautern where Iris lived. Being so close to the base, Faith Baptist was full of military personnel. From time to time top NATO officials would attend Sunday morning services, including General Harry Goodall, Deputy Commander in Chief of U. S. Forces, Europe, who at one time held two NATO commands. On one of these occasions, General Goodall, who was a member of Faith Baptist Church, heard Iris give her testimony and speak about where involvement with drugs always leads. Being concerned with the drug problem they were having in the schools on the US military installations, he asked Iris if she would be open to speaking in the schools located on the NATO bases. Sensing that this was a door the Lord was opening, she made herself available for this opportunity.

Only God could have orchestrated such a ministry on NATO bases for an ex-con not that long removed from the bars and streets of Houston, Texas. To do this, He brought a General into her life, and with his endorsement and the involvement of others such as Colonel Dan and Shay Butttolph, doors began to open across Europe, though at times it did take a special act of Providence. One of these occasions happened in Spain.

A miracle at Rota

It's a long way from Kaiserslautern, Germany to the Straits of Gibraltor on Spain's southernmost tip where *US Naval Station Rota* is located. Rota is the support base for the *US Sixth Fleet* and the *USAF Air Mobility Command*. It was also at that time one of the bases where Nuclear missiles were being housed.

When Iris left K-town for Rota she had the beginnings of a sore throat. The multiple stops and many train changes as she travelled across Germany, France and Spain did not help her condition and by the time she reached the town of Rota that evening she was sick and could hardly talk. She checked into a hotel, hoping and praying that by morning she would be feeling better. She wasn't, and the schedule had her down to speak seven times that day.

When she arrived at the Naval Base gate she could hardly talk. This turned out to be the least of her problems, however. What she didn't know was that this was the week of NATO's *Joint Military Exercises* and that all the bases across Europe had been put on high alert as they were expecting enemy attempts to infiltrate some of the bases, and the Rota installation in particular.

"I arrived at the heavily guarded gate and handed the officer my passport," Iris recalls. "He typed in my number, paused a moment, looked at me, then looked back at the screen, then turned to me again and said: *'Right. And you expect me to let you on this base?'* He motioned to a couple other officers to look at what had appeared on the screen. I knew what was happening because there is something in my passport numbers that alerts authorities that I am a felon; it doesn't give any details, it just registers that I am an ex-con. I knew I had to say something so I spoke up with my raspy voice. *'I know what you are thinking. Yes, I am an ex-con, but I've been invited to speak at the base schools today.'*

After discussing what they should do, one of the gate guards picked up the phone to call a superior officer. At that moment three black limousines appeared at the gate and a tinted window, in the middle car, was rolled down revealing the medals of a General. "*That's alright gentlemen, I'll take it from here. Miss Urrey,*" he said, "*please get in the car. I'll drive you to where you're scheduled to speak.*"

"You should have seen those guards snap to attention," Iris laughs. "I loved it. In just a few moments my emotions went from the lowest to the highest. This was a General who knew who I was and why I was trying to get on base. God had him there right on time. I feel badly that I can't remember his name."

When Iris was dropped off at the school her throat was still so sore that she thought it was bleeding. She threw herself on the Lord and ended up being able to speak at all seven of the assemblies. When she left the school later that afternoon, the General was waiting for her in his limousine. "*Iris, I'm taking you to see my wife. I heard part of what you have been saying and I want you to tell her your story.*" "*I will,*" she whispered.

"The driver drove us to the quarters where the General and another high ranking officer and his wife were staying. I shared my testimony. I told them what Jesus had done for me, but when I finished I didn't draw the net. This really bothered me the whole trip back to Germany."

When Iris finally did return to her apartment in Kaiserslautern several days later, an official-looking envelope was waiting for her. She opened it and read:

Thank you Iris for sharing with us. I gave my heart to Jesus last night.
Your friend,
Signed by the General

"I was thrilled," Iris recalls, "but I was still convicted that I had not made an effort to ask them that evening if they would like to receive Jesus into their hearts. I guess I was intimidated, but thank God He is the One who does the convicting and the saving, and He used my witness to reach a General. I promised God, however, that I would not miss another opportunity to invite people to turn their lives over to the Lord Jesus."

Witnessing—the "Iris-kind"

Iris' Kaiserslautern apartment was located not far from the train station where prostitutes worked their trade, a legitimate business in Germany. Iris saw her proximity to this activity as a witnessing opportunity, so it was not unusual to see her standing with them, sharing what the Lord Jesus had done for her.

Most of them spoke reasonably good English, as many of their clients were GIs.

While driving by the train station one day, Bob Ferguson, the pastor of Faith Baptist Church, was shocked to see Iris talking to a prostitute. *"What in the world are you doing, Iris? Don't you realize what people are going to think?"* He soon found out what she was doing when she started bringing some of the prostitutes to church.

Rain, sun, snow, freezing weather, those girls were always out there. "Sometimes when it was cold I'd prepare hot tea and spice bread and take it to them," recalls Iris. " I soon discovered that every one of them lived with the hope that the next person who came along would be the one who'd say, ' *'What are you doing here? Don't you want a different life? Will you let me help you?"* Down deep inside there lived a person who wanted to be different, just as I had longed to be a lady when I was chained by sin. They were waiting for that person who would really love them and take them away to live a new life. I told them about the One who had done that for me.

"One of the girls I got to know was a single mother who had children in school. She worked an eight hour shift during their school hours. All the girls had their shift hours, just like people who work regular jobs. My heart went out to them. I knew what they were going through. Only God knows what happened in the hearts of some of those girls. That's in His hands. I did what I knew I was to do. They of all people need to know about the One who truly loves them, but the church usually treats them like they'd treat a leper."

Doers Keep Opening

"...and a door was opened unto me by the Lord" (2 Corinthians 2:12b).

It's about a 5 hour train ride from Kaiserslautern to Kirkrade, Holland, and the *International Baptist Church* pastored by Larry Carson. Iris knew what the church had planned for her but she did not know what God had in store.

In attendance that Sunday were Colonel Dan and Shay Buttolph. If they had expected things to go as usual that morning, they were in for a surprise. There stood this tall attractive lady talking about her life of rebellion that had led to a life of crime and prison. Also attending the service that morning was the Buttolph's fifteen year old adopted son, Steven, who was always getting into trouble at school, and though he wasn't doing drugs, he was constantly getting into fights and showing serious signs of rebellion.

Iris was staying over that week for several additional speaking engagements, so the Buttolphs decided to invite her to have a meal in their home. They thought it might do their son good to have some time to interact with her and to have her share about where rebellion had led her. During the meal they talked about his being on his school's wrestling team and his success in cross-country races, something the parents had encouraged, hoping that this might take the place of his getting into fights. When they finished eating, the Colonel, his wife Shay, and their daughter Roshana, dismissed themselves to leave Iris alone with their son.

"I understand that you like to fight," said Iris, as she stood up. *"Yeah, I do,"* he replied. *"So do I,"* said Iris, as she gave him a push. He pushed her back. That's

121

all it took for them to start fighting. They wrestled all over the place. They ended up, out of breath, in the kitchen, where the Colonel and his wife had been waiting to see what the outcome of the "fight" was going to be. When Steven began to push and shove again, Iris picked the 15 year old up and threw him into a door that was half glass. It smashed into smithereens. Iris was so embarrassed she broke down in tears and it was not long before they all were hugging and crying.

A couple days after "the fight," the Buttolph's invited Iris back to their home where they gave her an envelope in which they had put $500 with a note saying: *"If you have a problem remembering our name, just think of "glass."*" Iris and the Buttolph family became close friends. In fact, Shay Buttolph immediately got in touch with the principal of the school on the NATO base where her colonel husband was stationed and it was not long before additional schools opened up at the recommendation of the Buttolphs. Eventually, Iris was even invited to speak at schools located on German NATO bases as well as at the French War College. In most of these situations, the schools provided her a room where she could counsel students who were having problems with drugs and rebellion.

The principal of one of these NATO schools was a Jew. He was not at all excited to have Iris address his student body and the only reason he agreed to have her was because of the influence of the Buttolph's. When she arrived, the principal made sure she understood the conditions under which she would be working. He took her into his office and said: *"Now listen, Miss Urrey. You can tell your story but if you start trying to convert the kids, telling them how much they need salvation, I'll stop you and you will never be invited back."* When Iris agreed to do what he asked, he said: *"When you're through, if they have any questions you can answer them, even if it is about your religion, but you can only do that in response to a question. If we're going to have religion preached here, I'll preach what I want. Understood?"* *"Understood,"* Iris said. What she didn't understand was how memorable this school experience was going to be.

The polka dot dress

For years Iris had wanted to wear a shirt-waist, navy blue, Swiss polka dot dress. She didn't know why, except that she had seen a lady wearing one and she liked it. There was no way she could buy one in a store that would fit her tall frame, so she decided to have one tailored. She knew someone who sewed, so she bought some inexpensive cloth. 'I don't know why I didn't buy the real thing," she recalls. "It wouldn't have cost that much more. Anyway, I took the cheap stuff to this lady and she made me my polka dot outfit in time for me to wear it at this school with the Jewish principal."

Because Iris often gets nervous when she speaks, she had the seamstress sew deep pockets in the sides of the dress so she'd have a place to put her sweaty hands. It was very hot that day and the gymnasium was not air-conditioned. Iris picks up the story.

"As I talked to the students I kept putting my hands in the pockets. When I was finished speaking I opened it up for questions and a little boy near the front was the first to raise his hand. He said: *'Did drugs turn your hands blue?'* I looked at my hands. The dress fabric was so cheap that the dye had turned my sweaty hands blue. *'No,'* I answered. *'Cheap fabric.'"*

The next question was about how Iris had ended her talk. She had said: *"The way I got off drugs was that someone introduced me to Jesus and I became a Christian.'* This student asked: *"If you're a Christian, why aren't you trying to convert us?"* *"That's a good question,"* she said. *"There is a story in the Bible about a man who asked Jesus for help. He had a servant back home who was sick and dying and he hoped that Jesus would heal him.*

"This man said something that surprised Jesus. He said: 'I have a lot of people who work for me. I have the authority to tell any of them to do anything and they will do it. I can say to them, 'go' and they will go. I can say, 'come,' and they will come. Jesus, you are a man under authority. You don't even need to come to my house to heal my servant. I believe you can speak a word from right where you are and my servant will be healed.'

"When I came here to speak to you, I put myself under the authority of your principal. What he says I can do or can't do, I obey. I am under his authority because he is in charge of this school." (Iris saw the principal standing in the corner at the back, watching and listening). *"One time, Jesus said that there is no greater faith than a person under authority. I could have gotten up here and started preaching to y'all. I could have taken advantage of the situation and done what I might have wanted to do and not put myself under the authority of your principal. If I did that I would never see you again. But, if I do what he tells me to do he may let me come back. Now, I tell you what. If you'll meet me out by the flag pole I'll try to convert all of you."*

The principle thought that was funny. He started to laugh, and from that point on he invited Iris to speak to his students every school quarter for all

123

three years she was in Europe. After she and Blue were married this principal wanted both of them to come. He'd say: *"Why don't you go to the dining hall and sing some of them good ole Gospel songs?"* He gave Blue a pad and said: *"Any kid who wants to talk to you, write their name down and I'll get them excused from class. I'm going to tell the students that you are in room 101 and that Iris will be in room 201 for the girls. I want you to tell them everything they need to hear."*

A word of caution

"This experience shows what God can do when you submit to the authority of the person you are working under," continues Iris. "I am convinced that the reason many schools have been closed to Christian witness is not so much the devil, but it's well-meaning people taking advantage of, and abusing opportunities they have had in the past. We know some preachers who have gone into schools where they have been told that they could only do so much, but they've decided that *'God's opened the door for me,'* and they have fired with both barrels. The principal then gets into trouble and eventually the doors are closed." That Jewish principal ended up calling every DOD (Department of Defense) school in Europe to recommend Iris and Blue.

Czechoslovakia

"Dobrey dyen. Welcome to Czechoslovakia, my dear sister."

Like most countries in their part of Europe, the Czechs and Slovaks have faced numerous challenges to their sovereignty from invading and occupying forces over the years. These two cultures were joined to form one country, Czechoslovakia, in 1918. Then tragically, after an interval of 20 years, they were forced to live under the oppression of foreign powers for the next 50 years. This period began in 1938 when France, Britain and Italy signed the *Munich Agreement* which authorized the Nazis to occupy the strategic Sudetenland area of Czechoslovakia. The Czechs called this agreement, the *Munich Betrayal*, as they were not even invited to attend the conference.

With the defeat of Hitler, however, the Czech and Slovak people were certain they would again be free to pursue their hopes and dreams, but these hopes were soon dashed as they were sold out once more by those they thought were their friends and allies. This time it was to Russia and Communism, at the *Yalta Convention* of 1944. For the next 45 years, these dear people, known for their love of freedom, art and music, languished under the evil domination of an atheistic regime.

But God had not forsaken His own who lived in Czechoslovakia, and in spite of severe persecution, He enabled them to press on. Among these was Vlado Fajfr; (pron. *Fyfer*, *"y"* as in my) who, along with his wife Ruth, had invited Iris to visit them.

"Please show passport. Passaporta, please." The train had stopped at the Austrian-Czech border and Iris was sitting alone in the compartment with her five

pieces of luggage. One of the suitcases contained Bibles which she had placed on top of the contents, as she didn't want to be accused of smuggling. The immigration officers looked at the pile of cases, then as Iris handed them her passport, they asked her to stand up. Iris was wearing a large fur hat and fur coat that had been given her, and she was wearing high-heeled boots. She stood, and stood, and STOOD, all 6' 3" of her! Iris says she looked like a gorilla when you added in the high heels, the tall hat and the fur coat. She looked down at them, they looked at the suitcases, mumbled something, and left, without opening anything. When she arrived at her destination, the same two officers returned to help carry her cases off the train. *"That big woman,"* had certainly impressed them.

Iris did not know what to expect as she stepped onto the platform of the Usti train station that January, 1982. This was her first visit to a communist country. She had heard Manley Beasley often speak of the Scottish evangelist, James Alexander Stewart, who had had such a profound influence on him. But now, Dr. Stewart, who had led Vlado Fajfr to the Lord many years before, had been called home, and his widow Ruth was married to this Czechoslovakian lawyer, pastor, outstanding sportsman, and witness extraordinaire. This had roused Iris' curiosity, and with the help of Ruth Stewart Fajfr's daughter, Sheila, Iris had been able to contact them. This trip would prove to be but the beginning of a very close friendship and ministry relationship between Iris and the Fajfrs, a relationship that spanned the years and resulted in additional trips for Iris, and eventually for Blue, after they were married.

It would not take Iris, Ruth and Vlado long to discover how much they had in common. They shared a love for the Lord and a passion for souls that had cost Vlado severely over the years. During the period of Nazi occupation and all through the years of Soviet oppression, in spite of beatings, imprisonments, Doctor of Law credentials being suspended, and permission to preach being withdrawn, he would not be dissuaded from being God's light in the midst of darkness. The authorities could not hold him down, as hard as they tried.

"Dobrey dyen. Welcome to Czechoslovakia my dear sister. Ruth and I have been looking forward to your visit. Oh, I see you have many bags. You are staying for long time?" Vlado and Ruth would soon learn that most of Iris' "cargo" were gifts, food and cooking items. These latter, especially, were treasures to folk who could find so little on the store shelves where they shopped.

She had not been in the Fajfr's home long before she was introduced to what Believers face on a daily basis in lands where Christianity is all but banned, and where any misstep can result in arrest. There was a knock at the door. Iris noticed the startled look on Valdo's and Ruth's faces. Who could that be? They had notified the authorities that they would be hosting an American visitor. But there was no need to be concerned; it was a young Believer who had just shot a rabbit and he was bringing it to Ruth to cook for their guest. This would be but the first of several other Believers who would join them that evening for fellowship and prayer.

The next morning at 6:30, on her way to the kitchen for coffee, Iris passed Vlado's son, Daniel Fajfr, on his knees. He had been there since 4 o'clock, as was his custom. Iris recalls: *"The more I got to know Daniel, the more godly I found him to be."* Following the *Velvet Revolution* in 1989, God would use Daniel in the building of one of the largest and most dynamic congregations in the Czech Republic.

The surprises, ministry opportunities and miracles Iris experienced would in themselves fill a book. She encountered one of these surprises in a nursing home.

The old lady
Vlado took Iris to a nursing home specifically to meet an elderly lady whom he had gotten to know. The nursing home was nothing like you would find in America, but typical of what you would often see in any communist country. It was a multi-story building with no elevator, windows with no curtains or blinds, a mattress on the floor, a small table, a chair, and a 5 gallon pail for a toilet. Vlado asked the "old lady" to share her story before Iris told hers.

She began: "I grew up in Prague in the 1920's when it was the one of the major hubs in Europe. Back then it was considered to be one of the most beautiful cities in the world. I remember the magnificent bridges, the museums and art galleries. It was a place of joy and music. There were Bibles in almost every home and people went to church. Then there was the war when the Germans came, and after that, the communists took over. They confiscated our home, pilfered our paintings and pieces of art. I was left with nothing. I couldn't even find my family. I was alone and I was scared.

"Then one day I began to remember something I had memorized as a little girl. I couldn't remember it all but I knew it went something like, *'Jesus wept...God loved the world...'*

I began to pray, '*Oh Father...for God so loved the world...for God so... Jesus wept.*' That's it, I thought. '*For God so loved the world that Jesus wept.*' God heard it as a prayer and He saved me."

Iris, who was in tears, was about to tell her story when the lady said, "*Since that day I have memorized 150 chapters of the Bible. Would you like me to recite my favorite one for you?*" At that she quoted all 21 verses of 2 Corinthians 5, the chapter that begins with...

"*For we know that if our earthly house, this tent, is destroyed, we have a building from God, a house not made with hands, eternal in the heaven.*" (NKJ).

After telling her story, Iris, not wanting to be completely outdone by someone almost three times her age, said, "*Let me sing some of my favorite scriptures for you. I find it easier to remember them when they're set to music.*" At that she began to sing, and sing and sing...

Note: When Iris returned to her home in Phoenix, Richard Jackson, pastor of the North Phoenix Baptist Church, asked her to share about her trip to Czechoslovakia in the Sunday morning service. He told her, however, not to tell the story of the lady in the nursing home as he was going to use it in his sermon. That morning Dr. Jackson spoke on, *God so loved the world...that Jesus wept.* Scores of people responded to the altar call.

Creative witnessing
During Iris' first trip to Czechoslovakia someone in one of the towns transcribed her testimony into Czech, and since it was against the law for citizens to own a copy machine, hundreds were then hand-copied and handed out as a witness. When she and her husband, Blue, returned to that particular town several years later, they discovered that Iris' testimony was still being circulated over that region of the country. Then, when they heard Blue's own incredible story they began copying it also. Hand-copied testimonies became a witnessing tool for some "more courageous" believers during the days of communist rule.

In one of the cities, the news had spread by word of mouth that two young Americans were going to be speaking at a meeting to be held in the basement of a house known to Believers as a "secret" gathering place. By ones and twos they arrived. Most of them were students who, just by their being there, risked losing the possibility of continuing their schooling, or even imprisonment if they were caught. The meeting began with two hours of prayer, then Iris and Blue shared their testimonies through an interpreter. Again, these were transcribed, and again, multiple hand-written copies were made for witnessing.

A special memory Iris has is that of Vlado Fajfr taking her to a "registered" church in the middle of the day, where they found people kneeling at the altar, praying. As she and Vlado watched, Iris thought she heard one of them repeat the name, Manley Beasley, several times. She whispered to Vlado who affirmed that several of them were praying for Bro. Manley. They were praying for his healing, that he'd continue to be used of God, and that he would be faithful to stand on God's Word and preach the truth. When Iris returned to the States, one of the first things she did was call Bro. Manley to report on the trip and to tell him about the prayer meeting. He was very moved to think that brothers and sisters so far away would be interceding for him.

Those were difficult, but purifying days for the church. There is a depth of commitment in the persecuted church that is not always found in parts of the world where it costs little to profess Christ.

A long-awaited freedom
Soon after the Velvet Revolution of 1989 that saw the non-violent overthrow of the Communist government, Blue and Iris were invited by the Fajfrs to return to Czechoslovakia. These were days of change and adjustment for everyone, including, or especially, Christians, whose witnessing for over fifty years was basically limited to when Believers gathered. There were, of course, the exceptions, like Vlado, who never was intimidated by the threats of government officials.

Now, however, even though the church was free to witness outside the walls of their meeting places, many believers were still hesitant to "go public." They were not sure how to best use this new-found freedom. Then came Iris and Blue. Out on the streets they went, into bars, restaurants, sharing their testimony and inviting everyone to the meetings where they would be speaking and singing each evening. And the people came. Among those Blue and Iris invited was a young Czech who had turned Communist and had risen through the ranks of the Russian military to a top officer's position. Now that Communism had been overthrown, however, he found himself among the most isolated and lonely people in the city. Many treated him with disdain, considering him to be a turncoat.

The church leaders had asked Iris to extend an invitation at the end of each service, something that the Czechs churches were unaccustomed to doing. That evening, after Iris had given a simple explanation of the plan of salvation, she led those who felt convicted of their need of a Savior to repeat after her a prayer of repentance and confession. When she asked those who had prayed that prayer to step forward, so many did so that she felt they must have misunderstood her; so she asked them to join her, Blue, and the church leaders, in an adjoining room. Among those who were standing at the front was this young military officer.

Iris and Blue went immediately to speak to him, and with Jana (pron. Yana) Fajfr interpreting, they carefully again went through the plan of salvation. When they finished, he said: *"I want proof. I want proof that there is a God and that He has a Son who died for me. I have been taught all my life that there is no God. I need proof."* *"Well,"* said Iris, *"my husband and I are proof that Jesus loves you. We came all the way from America to tell you about Jesus."* *"That's not enough,"* he replied. Suddenly, pointing to Jana, Iris said: *"Here's proof that there is a God. Jana Fajfr loves you. Tell him, Jana. Tell him you love him."*

Looking into his eyes with a compassion that only God could give, Jana said, *"I love you,"*
"So what," he replied.
"But," said Jana, *"I love you even though you and your Communist Party put my father in prison for years. You beat my father so badly that my mother died of a broken heart. You gave my brother all kinds of trouble and our whole family suffered for all those years because of your communism. I should hate you, but I love you, because God loves you."*

With that, the young officer broke down, Iris recalls. "Jana began to cry. Blue and I were crying. It was an awesome moment as we watched the scales fall from the eyes of a young confused, communist officer, as his allegiance to Christ was won by love."

This young officer would become an active member of the Usti church and is, to this day, serving the Lord.

A church plant
In the church and out of the church, Iris and Blue continued witnessing. Some said that they were turning the town of Usti upside down. The Usti believers had been praying about planting a church in the neighboring town of Dubi, known for its bars and nightclubs. They had held several services in

the park, so one was planned where the Blues would share their testimonies. On Saturday, when almost everything but the Dubi bars were closed, to the bars Blue went, with Daniel Fajfr as his interpreter. This was a new experience for Daniel who had never been inside a bar.

Blue passed out invitations to the open air meeting, sculptured balloon animals, and in his booming voice witnessed to everyone in one bar after the other. That night one of the bartenders attended the park service. When he overheard that the church was looking for a building where they could plant a church, he told them about an abandoned property that could be purchased for as little as $6000.00

On Monday, Blue, Iris, the church leaders and the bartender went to investigate. They found a three story building with a dance floor on the 2nd level with hardwood flooring. There were two apartments on the 3rd floor and enough land for each of the church members to plant their own personal gardens. Iris and Blue made two phone calls back to America which, along with their own contribution, resulted in having sufficient funds to purchase the property. Dubi had a new church home.

Note: That bartender would soon turn his life over to the Lord and eventually become the youth director of the Dubi church. It had all started with a witnessing visit to a bar. God does work in mysterious ways!

But, we've gotten ahead of our story. We need to go back several years to when Blue entered Iris' life. Things would never be the same for either of them.

Part Three

Then
There Were Two

"Until death parts us we've been called
to honor one another,
Showing what God's love is like
by how we love each other.
Partners in the game of life, learning and adjusting,
finding in the testing times
God's faithfulness and blessing."17

Iris Meets Blue

*"Will you accept a collect call from someone named
Blue, in Tomball, Texas?"*

Duane Blue lived in a 1952 International School Bus he had converted into
his own "home on wheels." Whenever he wanted to move on, he and his
two 80 pound German Shepherds would hit the road with his three-wheel
"motor-trike" attached to the back. The "trike" was itself an attention-getter,
built from the ground up by Blue, and powered by a Volkswagon engine. He
delighted in riding around town with those two shepherd dogs sitting behind
him in two van seats, with a 20" woofer between them, blasting out Blue's
favorite rock music. You could hear them coming two blocks away.

He had hair down to his belt, a beard down to the middle of his chest, he
was 6' 2" tall and as strong as an ox. He arm-wrestled competitively and, as
he recalls, only lost one match in his whole life. He was constantly trying to
prove that he was a real man and the only way he knew to do that was to be
better in something, than everybody else.

"Maybe I can't read or write but I can hurt you better than you can hurt me," was
his philosophy. In spite of all that show on the outside, however, Blue was not
a violent person and he was very lonely on the inside. Then on Christmas 1984
things began to change. *"Don't bring any of your weirdoes home for Christmas
this year,"* Iris' brother, Ernest, had told her. *"I've got one for you who is as weird
as they come. He's working on a house-painting job with me."*

135

Blue had gotten to know Ernest Urrey at work, and when Ernest told Blue that he had a sister *"who used to be a thief and a liar just like you,"* Blue decided to accept Ernest's invitation to join him at his parent's home in Outlaw Bend, for Christmas. Blue just knew he was going to freak the Urrey family out, and Iris in particular. At least that's what he thought—but it wasn't going to work out that way.

An Urrey welcome

Mirrell met Blue at the door with a smile and a big hug. *"What on earth?"* he thought. He'd never been hugged like that before and, to his surprise, the rest of the family didn't react to his "mountain-man" looking figure; in fact they all acted as though nothing was out of the ordinary.

After a time of getting acquainted, the next hour was spent praising and thanking the Lord for His blessings, each one sharing a testimony of God's goodness. Blue listened. He was feeling very uncomfortable. Then came the gift-exchanging time which the Urreys always did on Christmas Eve. Gathering the grandchildren around her, Mirrell explained that it was the tradition in the Urrey home to give the first gift to their "honored" guest. She handed Blue his present. He opened it to find a recording of the *Bible on Cassette*. His response was not what anyone expected. He was insulted. He got angry. He turned on Ernest, accusing him of telling everybody that he couldn't read. As far as Blue was concerned they were making him look stupid by giving him a Bible he had to listen to. The evening went downhill from there. Blue decided to hit back.

"They're going to be sorry they messed with me," he thought, as he moved over to sit next to Iris. *"Your brother has told me all about you, sister. You're a heroin addict, a prostitute, you've had dozens of abortions, you've slept with the Bandidos, you've spent years in prison..."* Blue recalls calling her every filthy name he could think of. He did everything he could to hurt her, expecting her to break down and run to her room in tears. *"But when I got through, Iris just smiled at me and said, 'Yep, that's the story I'm going to share at church next Sunday morning. Why don't you come with me? You don't know the half of what I've done.'"* *"What's gone wrong?"* Blue thought. *"This woman's weird. She wants me to go to church? Well, I guess I might as well go and freak her out there."*

Blue began to plan what he would do. *"I decided to wear my dirtiest blue jeans and the t-shirt that was full of holes. On Saturday I went shopping for a plastic bird that I could put in my beard. I wanted to look as stupid as I possibly could because I knew if I looked like that she wouldn't take me to church when she came to pick me up at my bus. Well, was I in for a surprise!"*

Church?

As Iris pulls up in her car, Blue steps out of the bus. He lets his two German Shepherds loose, expecting Iris to react, but she doesn't blink an eye. *"Do you have a refrigerator in there?* she asks. *"How do you get water? Do you have a bedroom?"*

"This is crazy," Blue thought. *"This woman is acting as though there's nothing wrong with me. I can't shock her."* Still thinking there was no way she would take him looking like that, he said: *"OK lady. I'm ready to go."* Then she shocked him. *"Get in the car,"* she said. Before he knew it he was walking through the door of a church.

"I could hear the gasps as the people watched us walk all the way down the aisle to the front row. I was feeling uncomfortable even while I was enjoying shocking the crowd. After all the singing and stuff, they finally introduced Iris and she gets up and starts telling them about all the illegal things she'd been involved in. I couldn't believe it. I thought, *'You fool. You don't have to tell them the truth. Lie to them. Nobody can prove any of the crimes you committed. You look like an idiot. This has to be the most stupid woman alive.'* But when she finished, four or five people came forward and knelt at the altar.

Then the preacher said: *'If anyone here is a sinner...'* *'Duh,'* I thought. *'Who isn't?'* He continued: *'Do you want to spend eternity in heaven or hell?'* *'Now, that's a no-brainer,'* I thought. *'Who's going to stand up and say, I want to go to hell.'* I repeated the prayer the pastor asked all the sinners to pray after him. It was a prayer I had prayed many times before, in jail. I was always ready to choose Jesus when I was behind bars, but it had never meant anything."

After lunch, Iris took Blue back to his bus. As he opened the car door, she said: *"If you think you are saved, you're not. You didn't meet Christ this morning and I don't want to leave here with you thinking that you have. You're lost. But if you ever want to find out what it really means to know Christ, you can call me collect any time of the day or night. I live in Atlanta. Here's my phone number."* Iris handed him her calling card and drove off. Blue thought, *"That's the last time I'll ever see her."*

A week later he walked down the street to a pay phone. It was 2:30 in the morning. He dialed her number and told the operator that he was calling collect. He heard Iris answer and he heard the operator say: *"Will you accept a collect call from someone named Blue, in Tomball, Texas?"* His heart was racing. She didn't hesitate. *"Yes, I will."*

This was but the first of many phone calls over the next couple of months. He began calling twice a week, then almost every day. He thought he would wear her down. He was testing her. One month her phone bill was over $700.00. Glenn Sheppard, who oversaw her ministry through the Home Mission Board of the Southern Baptist Convention, became very concerned and he tried to get her to refuse accepting what he thought was an excessive number of collect calls from Texas. Iris didn't feel she could do this, even though she hardly had any money left over after paying the phone bill. In light of this, Glenn decided she needed to be taught a lesson and had the phone cut off. To get it reconnected she'd have to come up with a $500.00 deposit. She didn't have the money.

Iris' next ministry engagement was in Titusville, Florida, where her friend, Peter Lord, was pastoring Park Avenue Baptist Church. That Wednesday night she asked the congregation to pray for the conversion of someone in Texas whose name was Blue. She told them what she basically knew about him and over 700 people stood to their feet and began to pray simultaneously. *"It sounded like a rushing wind,"* Iris recalls. Above the chorus of prayers she would occasionally hear, *"Oh God, save Blue. Oh God, tear down the strongholds of Satan in his life. Oh God, save Blue."*

Iris flew back to Atlanta that night on a "red-eye" flight. She arrived at her apartment around 3:30 AM, and as she opened her door, the phone was ringing. When Glenn Sheppard had told some folk about his teaching Iris a lesson, a woman in Conyers, GA took it upon herself to find the money to pay the $500.00 deposit and have the phone reconnected.

Iris picked up the receiver. It was Blue. He told her he had prayed to receive the Lord Jesus. That didn't impress Iris, however. She was not going to make it easy on him. She questioned the genuineness of his confession. She asked him: *"Where were you tonight at 7 o'clock?"* (That would have been 8 PM eastern time when the church in Titusville, Florida, was praying) He said: *"I was where I am every night; at the Brown Road Tavern. I smoked dope in the parking lot then went inside and drank rum and coke."*

Blue continued: *"Iris, I'm going to sell my bus and buy a house."*
"No you're not," Iris said, *"You're just going to keep driving around in that prison cell of yours."* This made Blue angry.

"Lady, you don't know who you're dealing with."
"Don't you get angry with me and try to prove you're a tough guy. You're nothing but a punk."
"If I could reach through this telephone I'd choke you."

"Before you try to prove you're a tough guy to me one more time, I've got a question to ask you. What would you do right now if you were standing in a church and a beautiful girl in a white dress said she was going to marry you and the preacher would look at you and ask, 'Do you take this woman to be your wife?' You would say, 'I do,' in front of witnesses. That's the law in our country. Then, what would you do when the preacher asked the woman if she would take you that she smiled and said: 'I want to spend the rest of my life with Blue. I love him so much and I want to be his wife, but every Friday night I'm going to sleep with Tim. I've dated him for years and it's become a habit. But after I sleep with him on Fridays, I'll go back to Blue on Saturday and be his wife for the rest of the time.'"

"Lady, you're crazy. I'd never marry anybody who's sleeping with someone else."
At that, Blue began cussing and yelling. When he cooled down, Iris said: *"You mean, you wouldn't accept her commitment?"* Blue yelled, *"That ain't no commitment. That's a bunch of garbage."*

Iris said: *"Well, what do you think God will do with your commitment?"*

In that moment, Blue began to understand where she was going. She was telling him that salvation was more than saying the words that you believed in Jesus, like a lot of people say; instead it's a change of life, it's leaving your old life behind and turning to go in a completely new direction. Finally he said: *"I think I understand. I want to pray."* Iris said, *"Alright."*

Now, here's Blue, standing in a phone booth in Tomball, Texas, phone receiver in hand, waiting for Iris to lead him in some kind of prayer—but nothing happened. Iris didn't say anything. He waited, and she didn't say anything. He kept waiting. His stomach was churning. He began to cry, and through the tears Iris heard him say:

"I don't know how to talk to God, all I know is that I'm sick and tired of the life I've been living and if God can do anything with me I'll do anything He asks me to do."

Blue tells folk that he now realizes that that wasn't a Baptist prayer, but he knows God heard his cry that night. He was changed. The next morning he dumped his booze, burned his dope, and started calling his two dogs by different names. What he had been calling them cannot be printed here, but now they would be known as Fatty and Skinny.

Blue went looking for the big thick, green, King James Bible Iris had previously sent him. He found it, told his dogs to take their seats on the trike, attached the Bible to the gas tank, then headed for the job site where he had been working. *"We've got to tell those creeps at the job what happened last night,"* he hollered back to the dogs. And that he did. *"I've come to tell you that I'm not going to be back. I gave my heart to Jesus last night and I can't hang around with junk no more. I'm headed for church right now."*

Iris had told Blue of a pastor friend of hers who had a church just a few miles from where his bus was parked. Blue, however, didn't know one church from the other so he stopped at the first one he came to. The door was locked. He knocked. A man in a suit answered.

"I've just met Jesus and I want to come to this church. Iris told me to contact you," announced Blue.
"I don't know who Iris is and you're not coming to this church," was the reply. *"Now, take your dogs and get out of here."*

So Blue and his dogs got back on the trike and headed for the next church down the road which turned out to be Central Baptist, the one Iris had told him to contact.

"I don't know much about Jesus," Blue told Charles Bullock, the pastor. *"I can't read the book Iris sent me but she said that you would help me learn. I'll do anything you want me to do. I'll go everywhere you go. I don't care what you'll be doing, I'll be there."*

The next morning Blue was back at the church by 8 AM, found the pastor's car, climbed in and waited for "their" first appointment. When Charles Bullock found him, he said: *"I can't take you to the hospital with me. You'll have to stay here."* Blue didn't move. Off to the hospital they went. After a few days of this routine it began to get to the pastor so, unknown to Blue, he phoned Iris. *"Iris, this guy's really obnoxious. Do you think you could get him to go to another church?"*

But Blue was not about to go anywhere, so the pastor decided to turn him over to Bobby Conners, the custodian, and they hit it right off. Bobby, a committed believer, took Blue under his wing and soon he would be building furniture for their church-sponsored school, painting, repairing the leaky roof, and helping in the many projects around the property that needed attention. God was using all of this to reprogram Blue to the new world he had just become a part of.

In the meantime, Iris had left on a four month around-the-world ministry trip with a group that included Jack Taylor and Glenn Sheppard. Before departing, however, she left a couple of contact addresses with Blue. Knowing how difficult it was for him to write, she really didn't expect to hear from him, but to her surprise, a letter was waiting for her in South Korea, and another in Germany—letters that took a good bit of deciphering to understand, though she really did know what was at the heart of them.

Heading Toward the Altar

"Will you?" "I will." "Will they?"

Though God had laid out Iris and Blue's future, a future that would have them joined together in marriage and ministry, getting "hooked" was not on Blue's agenda at the moment. Learning what it meant to walk with God was taking up all his time. Everything was different. This was proving to be "change" in the most radical sense of the word. God had a lot of work to do and Blue's heart was set on letting Him do it. He knew he could never look back. It would not be long before the inward transformation began to express itself outwardly—he started cleaning himself up. He cut his waist-length hair and shaved off his beard. He looked like a new person, which he really was. Little things in life were also taking on a new meaning. Past hurts were beginning to heal, such as the crushing emotions he had experienced for years on every Mother's Day.

"I hated Mother's Day. It was the worst day of the year. All it did was bring back memories of my own mother's suicide that I blamed on myself. But now, even Mother's Day, was beginning to have new meaning."

With Iris somewhere on the other side of the world, Blue went to the florist, purchased a dozen long-stemmed roses, mounted the three-wheeler, and with his dogs, headed for Outlaw Bend. If it were not for the motor-trike and the dogs, Mirrell Urrey might not have recognized the shaved, short-haired Blue when she answered the door; but the moment she did, he found himself again in the embrace of this woman who had loved him when he was so unlovable. *"Mama,"* he said. *"I have never liked Mother's Day, but because you have opened*

142

your heart and home to me, I have brought these roses as an expression of my love and thanks to you for all you've done for me." He was beginning to experience what it was like to be part of a family.

In the midst of all this, Blue was now finding himself looking forward more and more to Iris' return to the States. When she finally did get back home she invited him to join her for a speaking engagement she had scheduled in Atlanta, sponsored by Truett Cathy, founder and CEO of Chick-fil-A. Blue flew from Houston to Atlanta where he enjoyed being "wined and dined" by Mr. Cathy. It was a special time that would turn out to be but the first of other occasions when he and Iris would meet, and it was not long before they began seeing each other in a different light.

Will you? I will! Will they?

One beautiful autumn evening in October, 1984, seven months after he had been saved, Blue knelt down in a Houston restaurant and asked Iris to be his wife. When Iris responded with an *"I will,"* Blue went on to lay down two conditions that would need to be met if they were to marry.

"Iris, I don't want to do anything that will hurt your ministry because God is using you in a great way. I don't think that God is going to use me in the same way, so, if you agree, I'll go back into construction and will support and encourage you in everything God has for you. The second condition is that you speak to the men on your board and get their OK, and I'll go home and ask my pastor, Billy Crosby, what he thinks about our getting married."

Now, this may not sound very conventional, and it may seem as though they were getting things backward, but, very little was, or has been conventional in the lives of these two special servants of God. They received an affirmation from everyone they talked with; so now, all that lay ahead was deciding what kind of wedding they would have and when and where it would take place.

When a February date at First Baptist, Euless, TX was set, Marthé Beasley and friends began the plotting and planning. It was going to be quite an event—that is, until a December prison crusade, where Iris was scheduled to speak, was cancelled at the last minute because of a riot. With this date opening up on the calendar, and with a growing concern on their part that the wedding being planned was going to cost more than they felt should be spent, they decided to move the date up and get married the next weekend in the little Texas country church Iris' parents attended. But how do they break the news to those who had been planning for February? They called Bro. Manley.

With his support and blessing, they decided it best not to tell those who had been working toward the "other" date until after the fact, so arrangements were quickly made with the bi-vocational pastor of the Votaw Baptist Church near Outlaw Bend. The plan was for Blue and Iris to be in attendance at the Sunday worship service. Then, immediately after the final prayer the pastor would invite the wedding party to step forward as the flower arrangement on the pulpit table was exchanged for a wedding bouquet. This was of course a surprise to everyone there, other than for the Urrey family.

An amusing memory Blue and Iris will always have is of the pastor, who had broken a lens in his glasses that morning. There he stood, wearing one sunglass lens and one clear lens. He had to have glasses to read, so he had taken a lens from his prescription sunglasses and somehow attached it to his regular spectacles. Otherwise, all went smoothly, including the reception for which a lady in the church had baked a beautiful three-tier wedding cake, along with a chocolate groom's cake for Blue. But this wedding day was just beginning.

After the reception the newly weds rushed to the Houston Hobby Airport to catch a 6:30 flight to Dallas because Iris had agreed to give her testimony that night in a Ft. Worth meeting where Manley Beasley was speaking.

They were surprised to be met by Marthé who was still a little upset, having been told just that morning about the changed wedding plans. She would soon get over it, however, as she entertained Blue all the way to Ft. Worth. Following the service the Blues and all the Beasley family went out to eat, after which Marthé drove the newly wedded couple back to the airport to retrieve the luggage they had not had time to collect when they had arrived. But there was a problem—everything was locked up. They would have to return in the morning, so, Marthé, the chauffeur, drove them on to their hotel.

Next morning—7:30 AM.
Knock, knock, knock. *"Hello, hello. This is Marthé Ann. I've come to take you to the Mall. We're going to shop for some new outfits before you drive to Georgia. I'll be waiting."* They shopped until noon, an experience Blue remembers to this day, then, after finding their luggage and picking up the rental car, they headed for Georgia where Iris was scheduled to speak in another women's prison on Tuesday. And so the honeymoon continued...

Multiplied Grace

"My grace is sufficient for you, for My strength is made perfect in weakness" (2 Corinthians 12:9 NKJ).

The converging of two such strong personalities, with the amount of baggage each had been carrying for so many years, would normally be a prescription for failure. By God's grace, however, and with the prayer support and counsel of those who dearly loved them, Iris and Blue would persevere. They still had their moments along the way, when they themselves even wondered if they would ever make it.

The enemy can be expected to work overtime on those whom God is using, or is going to use to the degree these two trophies of grace have impacted His kingdom. He will work every scheme he can, to cause a fall, or to defeat God's children through discouragement. Sometimes he succeeds and sometimes it's a close call, but we can be assured that the devil never gives up. It's his mission to the end. One of these close calls happened about a year into their marriage. They were ready to call it quits.

"We were living in a trailer in Magnolia, Texas, " recalls Blue. "We had just had another big fight, so I called Bro. Manley who was in a meeting about 45 minutes away. I told him that we were probably going to get a divorce. He said that he would come as soon as the meeting was over that night. When I told Iris that I had phoned him, she hit the ceiling. She got madder than ever because she respected Bro. Manley so much and she didn't want to disappoint him. She was still mad when he arrived. As he walked through the door, she said: *'Well, have you come to referee?' 'No, sister,'* he said. *'I've come to take over. Sit down.'*

"I'll never forget what he told us. It was short and to the point. *'You two can just pull down those shades and live for Satan and be of no value to each other or the Kingdom of God, or, you can get right with God, and with each other, and go on to be of some value to Him. Blue, walk me back to the car. I'm going back to my hotel.'* I thought, *'Is that all he's going to do?' That ain't gonna help.'* Well, he did have something more to say to me personally when we got outside. *'Blue, there's one thing that you are going to have to learn about marriage, and it's this. Your mate is your heavenly sandpaper, but son, you've got a grinder.'*

"I got mad at him because I thought he was insulting Iris, that is, until he hit me with, *'In your case, Blue, sandpaper would never do the job. You need a grinder.'* With that he drove off. What Bro. Manley taught us that night has seen us through many rough waters since then, and God is still grinding away."

As iron sharpens iron, and as God's grace was being poured into their lives, they continued growing in their walk with the Lord and each other. It was clear by now that Blue would never return to the construction business because God had also called him into the ministry. Doors would open for them to share their testimonies, individually, and as a husband and wife team both in America and abroad.

Down Under

Norman Nix, president of the Mid South Wales Baptist Convention, and his wife, Marjory, were invited by Texas' Southern Baptists to attend their annual Evangelism Conference in the summer of 1987 where Iris and Blue shared their testimonies. What Norm and Marjory heard was something they felt could be powerfully used "down under," so they prayed, right there, about inviting the Blues to Australia. But how were they going to find them in such a large crowd? No problem with God who is in the business of divine encounters.

Back at their hotel, the Nixes pushed the elevator button and waited. The door opened and there stood Iris and Blue. *"We've just been praying about inviting you to come to Australia and here you are! Do you think you could come for 3 months?"* asked Norm.

It would not take long for the details to be worked out between Texas Baptists and the Mid South Wales Baptist Convention with whom a ministry partnership had just been established. Texas' Evangelism Director, Carlos McLeod, was excited to have his friends, Iris and Blue, be the first Texas envoys sent to the southern hemisphere under this cooperative endeavor.

During this three month assignment they ministered in prisons, schools, churches, indoors and outdoors, wherever the doors opened. The uniqueness of who they were and what they did was not lost on Australian media and soon they became headliner material in print, radio and television. They were considered celebrities. Television crews followed them to school assemblies and filmed their lectures on where drugs and rebellion can lead. In one city, what they shared at a school assembly was played in its entirety on the evening news. Their ministry was so effective that Iris and Blue were invited to return to Australia for a second and third time.

Though the Australian Baptist Convention arranged home-base accommodations for them at Sydney's Hyde Park Plaza, other than the expenses for the first trip being covered by Texas Baptists, Iris and Blue had to trust the Lord for the funding of the subsequent trips, which He miraculously did.

The Hyde Park Plaza management began taking pride in what Iris and Blue were doing. Each time they returned to Sydney from a ministry tour they would find newspaper clippings about where they'd been and what they had been involved in, tacked to the bulletin board so guests could keep up with their activities. To the surprise of the Blues, the hotel management also began upgrading their accommodations with each subsequent trip. Initially they had rented the least expensive single room available. The next time, however, they were given a two-room flat; then, on the last trip they found themselves occupying a Penthouse Suite with two bedrooms, living room and kitchen— all at the same price they had paid for the single room.

Heading home
It was May 30, 1987, and their flight wasn't scheduled to depart until 9:30 that night, so there was a whole day to say their farewells and to celebrate Iris' birthday, which just happened to coincide with their trip home. And celebrate they did.

The Nixes and other pastors gathered in the Blue's Hyde Park Penthouse Suite to celebrate. Blue had gone to *David Jones*, the fanciest store in the southern hemisphere, and had them bake a birthday cake with Iris flowers sculptured in the icing. To this, he added a beautiful bouquet of 50 live Iris flowers. What they did not plan on, however, was the large bottle of champagne, an appreciation gift from the hotel management. It was placed behind the door!

It is never easy to say goodbye to those you love, but for Christians, "goodbyes" are not final, as there is always the anticipation of another reunion, either in this life or the next. For Iris and Blue, even as they said farewell to their Aussie brothers and sisters, they were looking forward to stopping over in Hawaii the next morning where their friends, Colonel Dan Buttolph and his wife, Shay, were now stationed. They hadn't seen Dan and Shay since Europe where the Buttolphs had been so instrumental in opening up the NATO base schools to the Blue's ministry.

An unexpected surprise awaited them, however. Having crossed the *International Date Line,* it was still May 30, Iris' birthday, and this had not been lost on Dan and Shay. That evening they took Iris and Blue to a beautiful restaurant located inside an aquarium, where, while they were eating, a diver swam up to their table, holding a sign that read, HAPPY BIRTHDAY IRIS. He then stuck the greeting to the window. And, as if that were not enough, the next several days were filled with eating in the exclusive *Officers Club* in Pearl, reserved for full bird colonels on up. Dan Buttolph delighted in bringing high ranking officers to their table to meet them, intimating his conviction that their being in the Lord's army was of greater worth than that of this world's military. At one point they were even cleared to attend a Pacific Fleet briefing where the location of every US Navy ship in the Pacific theater appeared on a large wall-to-wall screen, along with the object of each mission. This in itself was a miracle, in that, due to Iris' ex-con status, she was not supposed to be given security clearance for anything military.

The fun, however, was just beginning. Colonel Dan provided them with, what he called, his "clunker" *MG Midget* to drive around the island. This was a spectacle to behold. Because they were so tall, the seats were pushed back, almost to the rear bumper, and with their heads sticking up above the windshield, they took off. Wind blowing in their faces, everywhere they went, they were treated with the utmost courtesy and favor as soon as the colonel's MG, that was well known on the island, was recognized. Lady Iris and Blue felt like royalty, which indeed they were—*Children of the King.*

Unexpected surprises such as these are sometimes hard to put into words, those extra blessings the Lord brings into our lives. There is a French Cajun word, however, that may come the closest. In southern Louisiana they might call what Iris and Blue were experiencing, "lagniappe." (pron. Lahn-yap) Lagniappe can be defined as an unexpected surprise, a little something extra like the cherry sitting on top of the whipped cream that is on top of the ice cream—that special something added to what is already wonderful.

Though God has surprised Iris and Blue with many *lagniappes* over the years, the most special was the one they were totally unaware of as they headed back toward the mainland—the *lagniappe* that was "in the incubator," the surprise the doctors had told Iris she was never to expect due to the number of abortions she had had over the years. But God, knowing the heart desires of His two children, overruled what supposedly was medically impossible and now, whereas "two Blues" had gone to Australia, "three Blues" were heading back home to America! *Denim Allen Blue* would, in approximately eight months, be joining his Mom and Dad, as two became three.

Dealing with Guilt

What can wash away my sin? Nothing but the blood of Jesus.
What can make me whole again? Nothing but the blood of Jesus.18

The birth of Denim was another sign to Iris of just how forgiven she was. The abortions she had had over the years had weighed heavily on her after she became a New Creation in Christ, and the enemy regularly used this to haunt her with memories of her past.

"My abortions became the biggest issue for me after I was saved. I would sometimes wake up in the middle of the night wondering if this one, or that one, was a little girl or a little boy, and who the daddy was. I wondered if, because of my many abortions, I would ever be able to actually bear a child. I would be overwhelmed with guilt. I'd sit on the edge of my bed and cry: *'Oh Lord, please forgive me. I'm so sorry I did it.'*

"Then one night it hit me. *'God's not the one who is bringing up my past, because He says in Psalm 103 that He threw all my sins behind His back in the sea of His forgetfulness and that He removed my sin as far as the east is from the west. If this is true,'* I thought, *'and God is not bringing up this stuff, who is? I'm sure not doing this to myself, and if I'm not, who is? There is only one other possibility—the devil.'*

"I always kept the Bible beside my bed open to the 20th chapter of John that tells the story of the empty tomb and the conversation Jesus had with Mary Magdalene. I can really identify with what Jesus did for her. I picked up my

Bible and read again how early in the morning Mary ran to the tomb and found it empty. *'That's it,'* I thought. *'That's it.'* I started talking out loud.

"'OK, devil, if you want to bring up my past, let me bring up yours. Early Sunday morning Mary ran to the tomb to anoint Jesus' dead body, but the tomb was empty. He was not there. He had risen. You thought you won, but you lost, sucker! If you want to wake me up again I'll tell you another story.'

"I went back to sleep. I had three full nights of sleep before I faced the same guilt again. At first I cried, then I thought—*I'm under the blood of Jesus. Devil, what are you doing under here? Oh, that's right. You aren't. You can't be under here because Mary ran to the tomb and when she got there it was empty, and it's still empty. You lost!"* I then slept for six nights before he came back—then two weeks—and now it has been years because I finally understood just how forgiven I was when Jesus saved me.

"Many Christians live with guilt over past sins because they have a problem believing just how forgiven they are. They struggle with how old things could really have passed away and how everything could really become brand new. They don't understand how new, 'brand new' is.

"When I had the Crossway Manor ministry, a girl came to us who was not only a prostitute and drug addict, but she was pregnant. It was not long, however, before she received Jesus as her Savior, and when she did, I started telling the girls that we were going to soon have a virgin birth. I didn't mean to be sacrilegious, but the way I looked at it was, if the sin that this girl committed in getting pregnant was washed away by the blood of Jesus, and if now it was as if she had never messed up, had never done anything bad, it was kinda like she was still a virgin.

"Now, I know that if you are already pregnant you don't get 'unpregnant' when you get saved, just like if you only have one arm, you don't automatically get another one when you are born again. Whatever you are physically before you are saved is what you will be after you are saved. You're going to have to wait until you get to heaven before you get another arm. But in the spiritual realm, when you are saved you become a brand new person. That was what I meant when I told this girl that in the eyes of Jesus she was pure, just as though she had never been touched by a man—just as if she was now a virgin.

"I also told the girls that being born again is just the beginning. It's the beginning of a process the Bible calls, *'the renewing of our minds.'* [19] It happens when God washes our minds with His Word.[20] If you have been doing drugs, living a sinful lifestyle, you've got to be reprogrammed—you've got to have your mind washed. This is not done by positive thinking or gritting your teeth, or any of that stuff; it's done by the Word of God that the Holy Spirit uses to reprogram us, to grow us up in our faith, just like what happens when we are born physically. We have to eat if we are going to grow.

"When you meet Jesus all your yesterdays are taken away. Your past is forgiven, but for you to experience this change in your daily living you have to eat spiritually so you will have the strength to fight off the attacks of the devil who is going to keep trying to lay a guilt trip on you by bringing up your past. This was where I struggled the most after I was saved. I had to get to the place where I could accept the fact that I was really forgiven, that my yesterdays really were gone and that all my abortions had been put under the blood of Jesus.

"There are many Christian women who have had abortions who keep being haunted by what they have done. The world tells them that it was just a fetus they got rid of, but in their hearts they know it was murder. They can't shake the guilt. This then leads to something else that many are having to deal with—how can they forgive themselves? This kind of guilt may not have anything to do with abortions, it may be forgiving themselves for other things like having lived a promiscuous lifestyle, having done drugs, abused alcohol, or done something else that they knew was wrong when they were doing it, but they did it anyway. I'm often asked: '*OK, I know I'm forgiven but I can't forgive myself. How were you able to forgive yourself?*'

"Well, my answer may surprise you. I haven't forgiven myself. I've read the Bible from one cover to the other and haven't found one place where it says I am to forgive myself. Nowhere. What I have found though, is that I am to believe on the Lord Jesus Christ and trust Him to forgive me. That's it. In the first place, I don't have the power or the right to forgive myself, because I am just a sinner saved by grace. The only forgiveness I can experience is the forgiveness I receive from the One who never sinned—the One who has the only right and power to forgive.

"I have been to the Holy Land 22 times. My main education has been travel. I've been around the world and have shared the gospel in both hemispheres. I've been to most of the places mentioned in the Bible but one of the most meaningful places to me is the Garden of Gethsemane where Jesus prayed just before He was arrested and went to the cross. One of these trips was right after I had done a Precept Bible Study. In this study, Kay Arthur says that when Jesus prayed, *'Let this cup pass from me,'* He was not saying, *'Please Father, don't let me die,'* as some people think He was saying, but Kay believes He was referring to the *Sin Cup* that He was going to have to carry to the cross. We all have a *Sin Cup*, we all deserve death; and Jesus, who never sinned, looked through time and saw me—He saw Iris Blue and He saw how full my *Sin Cup* was.

"In my imagination I hear Him saying: *'Father, do I have to take her cup? I've never taken drugs, I've never cussed, I've never sold my body, I've never stolen or lied. I've never murdered babies, I've never done all the sick stuff Iris did, and You want me to take her Sin Cup? Alright Father, not my will but Thine be done.*[21] At that moment, all of me, all my sins, all of them, were placed on Him who knew no sin. At that moment my Savior became sin for me, and when He died on the cross, carrying my *Sin Cup*, I died. The old Iris died! For God so loved me that His Son died, not just for me, but as me. When I knelt down on the sidewalk in front of *The Inferno* bar in Houston it was my time to get in on what God had done for me. My *Sin Cup* had already been passed to Jesus 2000 years ago, and what He did for me He has done for every person who has received the Lord Jesus as their *Sin-Bearer*—the One who carried their *Sin Cup* to the cross.

"That's how forgiven I am. That's how forgiven you are. Nothing else is needed to make you more pure in God's eyes. The debt of your sin was totally paid for 2000 years ago on the cross—*Paid in Full*—and the victory over Satan and his lies was completed on Resurrection Sunday. *'Death, where is your sting—grave where is your victory?'*" (1 Corinthians 15:55)

> *No longer can Satan accuse me, when He tries, it is nothing but lies.*
> *I tell him with each accusation, "The blood of my Savior applies!"*
> *Not only for now but forever, I am sealed by the blood shed that day,*
> *Forever, forever, forever, hallelujah, praise God I can say:*
> *"I'M FORGIVEN!"*[22]

"Every time the devil brings up your past; every time he tries to convince you that you are guilty of any sin that has been forgiven and placed under the blood of Jesus, remind him of his past.

'Devil, remember Mary? She ran to the tomb on Sunday morning and it was empty. You lost!'"

Two Families

*"Now, therefore, you are no longer strangers and foreigners,
but fellow citizens with the saints and members of
the household of God" (Ephesians 2:19).*

*"Iris, can you believe what we just saw? I didn't know there were churches like this.
This is where we need to be."*
"Well, what's keeping us from moving here?"
"Nothing, I guess. Let's talk with Bro. Jim."

Carlos McLeod, Director of Evangelism for the Texas Baptist Convention, had asked Iris and Blue to give their testimonies in a meeting he was to hold at Robinwood Baptist Church in Seagoville, Texas. Little did they realize what God had in store for them—here Denim would be born, and it would be here that a relationship would be forged with a pastor that lasts to this day.

What Iris and Blue had experienced in that first service was a bit out of the ordinary, though it should be the norm for any healthy church body. A man went forward during the invitation, expressing his desire to receive Jesus Christ as his Savior. After being counseled, he shared with the pastor that his wife had recently died, that he had two little girls to care for, and that he had just lost his job. Pastor Jim Everidge then turned to the congregation, explained the situation, and asked:

"What do you think we should do? A man jumped to his feet. *"I'll give him a job." "No way,"* called out another. *"You gave the last person a job. It's my turn."* Two ladies then stood and said that they would arrange to have evening meals

154

prepared for him and provide child care for his two little girls every week day.

This was the kind of church Iris and Blue wanted to be a part of, but if they were going to make a move it had to be done quickly as they were about to fly to Europe where they'd be ministering for the next 12 months. They decided that they only had time to move their church membership, so, several days before they flew to Europe they joined Robinwood Baptist, in Seagoville, Texas.

Their relationship to a church body has always been fundamental to the Blues' family and ministry life. They have never considered being just casual members. They have always poured themselves into the life and work of whatever church they've been a part of. In a day when many "itinerant" ministers are church members in name only, Iris and Blue, and now Denim, can be found right in the middle of whatever is going on in their church family—giving and serving. An interesting aside—while they were in Europe, they tithed to both their home church in Seagoville and the International Baptist Church in Brussels, Belgium, their home away from home that year.

Denim Blue
It was not only into the Blue family that Denim was born, but he was immediately "adopted" by the Seagoville congregation. He arrived at 9:45 AM on November 30, 1987, weighing in at 10 lbs. It was here, at Robinwood, that he and his parents would be surrounded by the love and care of an extended family made up of eternal relatives, children of the heavenly Father with one common heritage—heirs and joint heirs with His Son, the Lord Jesus.

Now, for Blue and Iris, things would never be quite the same again. The child they had dreamed of, the *lagniappe* of God's love, was now a reality, and with this addition would come the adjustments, at home and on the road, that have always been the common challenge to those in itinerant ministry. Denim would eventually begin his formal education at the *Pathway to Learning* School where he'd continue until Mom and Dad decided that he needed to travel full time with them in ministry. This, of course, meant another major adjustment—he would now have to be home-schooled.

Home-school Denim? No problem. Iris could do that with the help of materials available in print and on video. And while she was at it, why not include Blue who was still struggling with his own reading and writing? She would teach them together! And teach them she did, until both father and son matriculated about the same time.

Learning by travel
With all the challenges of learning "on the go," there were also the advantages that travel offered. They would experience first hand many of the things written in their history and geography lessons, which turned out to be the easier way for father and son to learn. This was later confirmed when they both were diagnosed as being dyslectic.

Ask the Blues about the Holy Land? Well, Iris has been there 22 times, Blue 12, and Denim, since he was eight years old, has visited the Land of the Bible every year but two. It was on one of these trips to Israel that his parents "accidentally" discovered that God had given him a beautiful voice and a fine musical ear. As the three Blues were leaving a pizzeria in Jerusalem, Iris spotted an ice cream stand across the street. She immediately broke into song: *"Thank you Jesus,"* to which Denim spontaneously echoed, *"Thank you Jesus."* Every line she sang, he repeated, and before they knew it they were harmonizing. And so it was that Denim entered the music ministry and it would not be long before he would be singing solos and sharing his own testimony that, to this day, is a very important part of his life and calling.

Moving east
1997 was a watershed year for the Blues. Their pastor, Jim Everidge, felt God leading him into his own itinerate ministry of evangelism. In addition to this, Texas Baptists had become divided over a number of issues which were causing tension within the Baptist community, and Blue and Iris had friends in both camps. Although they were simply wanting to minister wherever God opened doors, it was becoming increasingly difficult to do so, with some on one side telling them they shouldn't go here or there, while those on another side were saying just the opposite.

New pastor—New church
During this period, a friendship was developing with Johnny Hunt, pastor of First Baptist Church, Woodstock, GA. With his passion for souls and his down-to-earth approach to life, it was not long before their hearts were bonding with this *Lumbee Tribe Native* American. They knew they could just be themselves around him, which Iris had experienced on one occasion when she and Dr. Hunt were on a program together where hundreds of pastors were in attendance. After Iris had given her testimony, she sat down next to Bro. Johnny who was scheduled to speak as soon as the offering was taken.

The "appeal," however, went on and on and on until Iris could hold it in no longer. She leaned over to her future pastor and said: *"They sent me to prison for less than that." "Bro. Johnny almost came out of his seat,"* Iris recalls.

Dr. Paige Patterson invited the Blues to participate in the Southern Baptist Convention when it was held in Atlanta, and while in the area Dr. Hunt invited them to minister at the Woodstock church where they had already been on a previous occasion. While there, and with the encouragement of some of the members, they decided to pull up their Texas stakes and move to the Peach State where they would reside for the next six years.

Though their new church family was much larger than any they'd been a part of, with its thousands of members, the Blues would soon feel at home. Bro. Johnny gave them opportunities to minister, and Iris and Blue would use their considerable culinary skills to get to know the staff of over 100.

It had always been their policy to prepare a special Christmas meal for the staff of every church they'd been members of. This meant feeding everyone from the pastor, to the secretaries to the custodian and all their spouses. Up until this year, however, it had been quite manageable, with the largest staff numbering only eight. Now, having just moved into their 1500 sq. ft. house Thanksgiving weekend, they were faced with preparing meals for over 200, which would be a challenge, but not impossible. They had a basement! They would divide the staff, and their spouses, into groups, each assigned with a specific time to appear, beginning at 11 AM, over a three day period.

Everything was made from scratch. Blue was up at 3 o'clock each morning preparing his own special recipe of Seafood Gumbo made of shrimp, chicken, sausage, rice and a few other secret ingredients while, for those who did not like gumbo, Iris was making her own special vegetable and beef (the finest tenderloin) soup. Then, added to these was the "lack-nothing" salad bar, topped off by an 8' long dessert table. But that was not all. As the guests left, they picked up their special gifts, something for the men and something for the ladies.

This continued for the six years they lived in Woodstock. It would become one of the staff highlights of the season, and this expression of love and appreciation for those who serve them, is practiced to this day.

Returning "home."

It is said that Texans can never really feel at home living anywhere but in the Lone Star State, and when Iris and Blue learned that their former Seagoville pastor, Jim Evridge, had begun planting a church in Lucas, Texas, they felt that it was time to head back west and get behind their friend in this new challenge. So move they did, back to the land of the big sky, to join their hearts with a new family known as Cornerstone Baptist Church.

To be Continued...

*"Brethren, I count not myself to have apprehended; but this
one thing I do, forgetting those things which are behind, and
reaching forth unto those things that are before, I press toward
the mark for the prize of the high calling of God in Christ Jesus (Philippians
3:13-14).*

Like a work in progress, a mosaic yet to be completed or a piece of pottery being shaped in the Potter's hands, so is the life of a pilgrim who is still pressing on. Whereas most biographies chronicle the life of someone who has completed their earthly journey, this is the story of one who still has more roads to travel, more mountains to climb, rivers to swim, and more lessons to learn. Yet unwritten are the days that lie ahead for Iris. As is true for all of us, her future waits as an unfinished painting. Only the Artist himself can visualize what the completed work will look like.

The late Christian statesman, Dr. Harry Ironside, used to tell the story of a noted artist who had been commissioned to create a large mural. He erected a scaffold and proceeded to put the background of the mural on the wall. A friend, entering the studio, stood quietly at the back of the room not wanting to disturb the artist who was preoccupied in covering the wall in dark gray and deep blue tones.

Wishing to view what he had done from a better perspective, the artist descended the ladder and moved backward toward the door, never taking his eyes off the mural. He was so intent on studying his work that he backed right into his friend, to whom he enthusiastically explained: *"This is going to be the masterpiece of my life! What do you think of it? Isn't it grand?"* His friend replied, *"Perhaps, but all I see is a great, dull, daub of paint."*

"Oh," said the artist. *"I forgot. "When you look at the mural you can see only what is now there, but when I look at it, I see what it is eventually going to be , and that makes the difference."*

Finishing well

Though there is always the danger of detours, times of stumbling and failures of trust, as is true for all pilgrims, if the past is any indicator of the future, Iris will continue following hard after her Lord, living "on the edge," as some put it. She will never be satisfied to not have to trust God for everything pertaining to her life. She has never forgotten the question Manley Beasley would often ask her, *"What are you trusting God for, that if He doesn't come through you'll be sunk?*

In the prayer to His Father in John 17, the Lord Jesus said, *"I have brought you glory by completing the work (finishing the assignment) you gave me to do."* The Apostle Paul, as he neared the end of his journey, said, *"I have fought the good fight. I have finished the race. I have kept the faith"* (2 Timothy 4:7 NKJV). The aspiration of Iris Urrey Blue is to finish well, to hear at the end of her journey, *"Well done, good and faithful servant..."*

So it is in faith that we all join her in looking to the future and the race yet to be run—for the painting yet to be completed by the Master Painter who holds our futures in His hands. And as we do, we take comfort in the reminder found in the letter to the Hebrews, the reminder of where the secret to finishing well lies.

"Wherefore seeing we also are compassed about with so great a cloud of witnesses, let us lay aside every weight, and the sin which doth so easily beset us, and let us run with patience the race that is set before us, looking unto Jesus, the author and finisher of our faith, who for the joy that was set before Him endured the cross, despising the shame, and has sat down at the right hand of the throne of God" (Hebrews 12:1-2 NKJV).

Epilogue

Our story opened with a *Foreword,* a tribute, by one of Iris' beloved, former pastors, Johnny Hunt. Now we close with a testimony by Jim Everidge who, at this writing, has known the Blues for over two decades and has been their pastor for a total of sixteen years—first in Seagoville, Texas, and now in Lucas. Bro. Jim sums up well what those of us who have known the Blues over the years have observed. But this is not only a look back, it's a testimony of the present and, by God's grace, a picture of the future as Iris, Blue, and Denim continue to fulfill the calling God has placed on their lives.

A Pastor's observation

"I preached a message one time on *The Gospel According to the Blues.* They were not present. I used Acts 4:13, that *"when they* (Annas the high priest, Caiaphas and others) *perceived that they* (Peter and John) *were unlearned and ignorant men, they marveled and they took knowledge of them, that they had been with Jesus. "*

"One of the things I have learned from the Blues, and continue to learn, is that when you have truly been with Jesus you are going to have *a lop-sided lifestyle*—you are going to live for Jesus. Also, when you've been with Jesus you are going to have *a limited vocabulary*—all you want to talk about is Jesus. Then, when you've truly been with Jesus you're going to have *tunnel vision*—you're just going to see Jesus. I pray that their tribe will increase. Oh how we need more of the kind of Christians the Blues are in our churches today!

"The religious leaders didn't perceive that Peter and John had been with the doctors or teachers of that day. They didn't perceive that they had been with convention leaders or famous personalities; they perceived that they were unlearned, but that they had been with Jesus. That's what blesses me when I think of Iris and Blue. You can't say that about a lot of people.

"Their faith is contagious, not contaminating. The writer to the Hebrews says that we ought to be a blessing to our spiritual leaders, our pastor, and not a burden. I've pastored for many years and have discovered that a lot of people look better going away from you than they do coming toward you. When you see Iris, Blue and Denim, coming, they look good.

161

"My life verse for them as a family is, 2 Corinthians 5:17, *"Therefore, if any man be in Christ, he is a new creature..."* If people don't believe that God can make a change in a person's life they have never met Duane and Iris Blue.

> *I'd rather see a sermon than just hear one any day.*
> *I'd rather one should walk with me than merely tell the way.*
> *The eye's a better pupil and more willing than the ear,*
> *Fine counseling's confusing but example's always clear.*
> *For I might misunderstand you and the high advice you give,*
> *But there's no misunderstanding how you act and how you live.*[23]

"Talk is cheap in America, and that is as true in the church—from the pulpit to the pew. The thing about Duane and Iris is, what you see is what you get.

"The other verse I relate to Iris and Duane, as their pastor, is Philippians 1:21—*"For to me to live is Christ and to die is gain."* The dying bit at the end of that verse can come at any moment, but I'm talking about the living part. I've watched them, and I can truly say from what I've observed for over twenty years of knowing them, is that Christ has been **the source of their life.** We know that, generally speaking, Jesus is the source of all life, whether it is physical or spiritual, but in practice Jesus has truly been the source of their lives, spiritually.

"When Iris and Blue got saved, they didn't meet a church, they met the living Lord. 1 John 5:12 says that, *"He that hath the Son hath life; and he that hath not the Son of God hath not life."* One of the ways you know you have met the Son is that you will have spiritual life. The **source** of their lives, all through their ministry, has been Jesus.

And **the strength of their life has been Jesus,** in good times and bad. They have proven that they can do all things through Christ who strengthens them. But not only that, God has been **the supply of their life.** Philippians 4:19 promises them that their God shall supply all their needs according to His riches in glory in Christ Jesus. As itinerant missionaries Jesus has had to meet the needs of their lives and He has done exceedingly above any of us could have wished or thought. I've seen two people who have lived by faith and Jesus has had to be the supply of their life.

"Finally, I've seen Jesus be **the song of their life.** Paul says, *"Rejoice in the Lord always, and again I say rejoice"* (Philippians 4:4). Iris has had but one song, and it has been about Jesus. She has sung it everywhere they've gone around the world! What can you say, other than, *Hallelujah, praise the Lord for lives that are sold out to their Master!"*

Appendix

Tributes

For almost four decades First Southern Baptist Church, Del City, Oklahoma, hosted an outdoor summer crusade called STARLITE. This crusade annually featured the finest speakers, vocalists and singing groups from across the nation. Thousands of people testify to having first met Christ at STARLITE.

Each year's crusade would also be highlighted by testimonies from individuals whose lives had been touched by the Lord in a remarkably significant fashion. Iris Urrey was just such a person. When she stepped to the platform on a sweltering summer night the restless crowd immediately calmed, eager to hear the testimony of the rough street woman who, by God's grace, had become a gracious lady. The bleachers became a quiet cathedral under a starry canopy as the crowd strained to hear every word. They were riveted to Iris as the love of Jesus flowed from her heart out into the stands.

From that night on, Iris became a frequent guest at First Southern, joined later by her husband, Duane (Blue), and still later, her son, Denim. As a pastor, my heart rested confidently in the integrity and authenticity of the Blues. I cannot tell you how often I heard the words, *"They are just like me. If God can do it for them, He can do it for me as well."* It is difficult to describe the winsome, magnetic appeal of their lives, except in terms of the grace of God—and isn't He the only hope for us all.

—**Tom Elliff**: *Author, speaker, president of Living in the Word Ministries*

Iris Blue is a woman on fire for her Lord. She had a miraculous conversion and has never forgotten it! Her testimony is not only an amazing example of God's grace but also a motivating impetus for every woman to be all God called her to be—whatever her strengths or weaknesses. I am inspired every time I hear her.

—**Dorothy Kelley Patterson:** *Southwestern Baptist Theological Seminary, Ft. Worth, TX*

God's grace is a marvel. Iris was a fun-loving, tough, mean, licentious, female hell-raiser until Jesus won her heart. Jesus made a doubly fun-loving, tough, sweetheart—holy and pure before God, a gracious female heaven-raiser with a fire in her bones to see people come to Christ and honor God.

—**Paige Patterson:** *President, Southwestern Baptist Theological Seminary, Ft. Worth, TX*

In my 28 years of ministry, no one has quite impacted my life like Iris Blue. Through her simple humility and incredible story of transformation, she has inspired and challenged me to become a more passionate Christian leader. More importantly, she has modeled a lifestyle of commitment to Christ and the change that only comes through the cross of Calvary. I have ministered with her in many settings, and I have seen her story melt the hearts of the proud and lift the hopes of the lowly...and shake up the lives of every one in between! She is one of God's great servants and I consider it an honor to call her my friend.

—**Lavon Gray:** *Minister of Music and Worship, First Baptist Church, Jackson, MS*

Iris came to Canada to speak in several Conferences on Revival when I was the Director of Evangelism for the United Baptist Convention of the Atlantic Provinces. Every time she was with us our people were soundly blessed and challenged.

On one of these trips, she flew into Halifax from Brussels, Belgium. As we were waiting for her, to our surprise, we were notified that immigration officials had arrested her. We soon discovered that an immigration officer had read the announcement I had put in the paper about our hosting an ex-convict from the United States and he had notified all the ports of entry to be on the lookout for her. After some negotiating, phone calls and prayer, they finally let her through. And what a blessing she was as God used her again, for His glory.

—**Jeff Brooks:** *former pastor, director of A Certain Sound Ministry, Knoxville, TN*

I remember hearing about Iris shortly after her conversion experience. I waited a while, however, before inviting her to speak at one of our *Great Hills Ladies' Retreats* in Palacios, Texas, where we all were enthralled by her testimony. On the way home to Austin, one of my ladies asked, *"What is a pimp?"*

A couple years later Iris was our guest speaker at a large ladies retreat at the *Falls Creek Encampment* in Oklahoma. Our oldest daughter, who was not walking with the Lord, was there. In a private conversation Iris asked Jennifer if she was sure she was saved. Praise the Lord for her discernment. That question continued to haunt Jennifer until the next week, alone by her bedside, she knelt down and asked Jesus to save her. She was baptized several weeks later. Iris, we will always be in your debt.

—**Barbara O'Chester:** *Founder and retired director of the Great Hills Ladies Retreat Ministry, Austin, TX*

I remember meeting Iris in 1978 at a Parent Teachers Association meeting. It was not a pleasant experience. Iris was a new believer and had not been out of prison very long. Unfortunately, I was suspicious, judgmental, and critical. As the pastor of our county seat First Baptist Church, I was embarrassed at Iris' use of the English language which reflected eight years of imprisonment, and many years of rebellion.

When the session ended that night, a large crowd of parents surrounded her. They had hung on every word she'd shared from her converted heart, and they were eagerly asking her, *"Can you help me with my little girl?" "What kind of advice can you give me for my teenagers?"* I was beginning to see how God was already speaking through her, and over the next three decades I have never ceased to be amazed at how He has continued to use this humble servant in incredible ways. Fortunately, I got over my initial shameful, self-centered embarrassment and soon Iris was sharing her testimony in my own church. Lives were forever changed.

When my wife, Linda, and I became missionaries to Germany, we invited Iris to join us for a series of speaking engagements at the International Baptist Church in Stuttgart, where I pastored. God revealed Himself in awesome ways through her and continued to do so after she and Duane were married. The two of them traveled to Europe several times over the years to share their lives, faith, and witness in our EBC churches. Many lives were transformed.

I recently invited the whole Blue family to Lubbock, Texas, where I now serve as the Director of Missions for Lubbock Area Baptists. They ministered in nine of our churches in four days. God moved. Heaven came down. Need I say more.

—**Larry Jones:** *Director of Missions, Lubbock, TX area Baptist Association*

"Mister, if this plane falls out of the sky, do you know for sure you're going to heaven or are you going to hell?" This was the question that greeted me as I stepped out of the restroom on the L1011 heading for Switzerland. I looked up into the face of a woman who towered at least six inches over my head. I knew she wasn't the kind I would want to argue with.

"I'd go to heaven," I answered. *"What about you?"*

"My name's Iris, and if this plane goes down, I'm going to heaven."

For the next ten minutes we stood in that tiny alcove as she told me her story—how far she had strayed from the Lord and how He had transformed her life. I was mesmerized. Upon returning home I told my wife, Jackie, about Iris and we decided to invite her to visit us in Atlanta where I was Special Assistant in *Prayer for Revival and Spiritual Awakening* at the Home Mission Board of the Southern Baptist Convention. This visit led to our inviting Iris to give her testimony at our national conferences. During this period she would become a *Mission Service Corps Volunteer* with the Home Mission Board, now the North American Mission Board, a relationship she has maintained for the last 28 years, making her the longest living MSCV.

Iris will forever be in our hearts and in the hearts of our children. Her story has touched so many lives over the years, as it has ours. We will be eternally grateful to call her our sister and friend.

—**Glenn Sheppard:** *Director, International Prayer Ministries, Conyers, GA*

Notes

(Endnotes)

<u>Chapter One</u>

1. Punkin would sometimes go with her parents to visit Iris. Her older two siblings, Ernest (Jug) and Rebecca (Jo), visited her once during the 8 years of imprisonment.

2. A film, *The Goree Girls,* starring Jennifer Aniston, is to be released in 2010.

<u>Chapter Two</u>

3. *Is Your Salvation Real or Counterfeit?* Available from www. duaneandirisblue.com or Debbieebeasley@yahoo.com

<u>Chapter Four</u>

4. *Bandidos Motor Cycle Club* (sometimes spelled Bandito), also known world-wide as the *Bandido Nation* with 210 chapters in over 16 countries. Founded by Don Chambers, Vietnam Marine veteran, in 1966 in Texas, it is listed by the FBI as an *Outlaw Motor Club.* They are rivaled only by the *Hells Angels* in size and criminal activity, with whom there are regular turf wars resulting in multiple murders. Don Chambers, their founder, was eventually sentenced to life in prison, but word has it that he did put his faith in Christ before he died of cancer.

5. *Old Lady* was the term used for the Bandido girl friends who were usually in their teens or twenties. Iris rode with the Bandidos between the ages of 15 and 17.

<u>Chapter Six</u>

6. A prison "tank" is a *ward* with 8 bunks or more. There may be as many as 40 of these on a floor, 20 on either side of a hallway.

7. Terizin was a WWII Nazi concentration camp NW of Prague, Czechoslovakia, where, between 1941 and 1944, Jewish musicians, writers, artists and more than 15000 Jewish children were held captive before being moved on to Auschwitz for extermination. Though there was no formal schooling, the children were encouraged to paint and write. In many of their poems the children dreamed of a life they longed to experience but one they knew they would never know. Of the 15,000, only 100 survived.

Chapter Seven

8. Chaplain Olsen knew that in order to win Iris' trust he had to treat her more as an equal, than as a superior looking down on an inferior.

Chapter Eight

9. Words by Horace Gerlach. Copyright search on *Copyright.com* found no matches.

10. Iris' father loved his children but had never been able to say the words, *"I love you"* to any of them, until after Iris and Blue were married.

11. The seven years represented the time Iris spent in Goree. She was allowed to receive some gifts during her stay in the Harris County jail.

Chapter Thirteen

12. From the poem, *Missions Next Door* by Ron Owens © 1978 ICS Music

Chapter Eighteen

13. Author unknown.

Chapter Twenty

14. From the hymn, *He Leadeth Me,* words by Joseph Gilmore

Chapter Twenty-one

15. There are presently over 2000 serving in this capacity

Twenty-four

16. From the hymn, *Wherever He Leads I'll Go,* by B. B. McKinney © 1936, renewal 1964, Broadman Press

Part Three

17. From the poem, *Until Death Parts Us* by Ron Owens © 1995 ICS Music

Chapter Thirty-one

18. Words by Robert Lowery

19. Romans 12:2

20. Ephesians 5:26

21. Matthew 26:36-46

22. From the poem, *Forever Forgiven* by Ron Owens © 1989 ICS Music

Epilogue

23. First verse of the poem, *I'd Rather See a Sermon,* attributed to Edward A. Guest

Photos

Pat and Mirrel Urrey with family. Joe, Ernest, Iris, and Punkin with little Tara.

Blue (Duane), Iris, and Denim

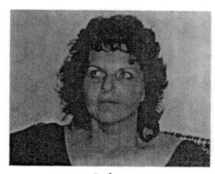

Before.   After.

Iris with Tara and Danny Green and their children Forest, Emerald, and Hunter.

Iris with her "little sister" Punkin (Evelyn).

Iris at age six.   Card from prison.   Blue and Iris.

Iris and Blue with Israeli soldier in Hebron Israel.

Mike Huckabee and Iris reuniting after many years.

Ron Owens with Iris.

Iris with David Owens, Debbie Beasley at an International Congress on Revival in Interlaken Switzerland.

Drinking from Jacob's well with Jamal, the well-keeper, and her pastor, Jim Everidge.